Basics of Christian Thought
Todd Brennan, General Editor

Volume One
SOURCE

What the Bible says about the
problems of contemporary life

John L. McKenzie

THE THOMAS MORE PRESS
Chicago, Illinois

The material herein has appeared in different form in the newsletter of the same title published by the Thomas More Association.

ISBN 0-88347-172-8

Contents

Publication of this volume of
BASICS OF CHRISTIAN THOUGHT
is made possible in part by a
ROBERT E. BURNS GRANT
from the Claretian Fathers and Brothers

INTRODUCTION

THIS book is written in response to a suggestion made by the staff of the Thomas More Association. The decision to write it was not made without discussion and reflection, and consideration was given to objections. Many of these objections arose from purely personal considerations which I feel no obligation to rehearse here. Others are less personal and more serious and a review of some of them will serve both to introduce the reader to the book and to set forth some of the values which we hope it will realize.

The obvious objection to a book which will attempt to review biblical thoughts and sentiments on a wide range of contemporary problems is not personal; it would be raised against any author. The book seems to be a rather explicit attempt to establish the author as a kind of *guru*. I rebelled against assuming this role. But it was urged that a feeling of modesty should not keep me from doing something worth doing; that probably no one else would do it (because they think they have more worthwhile tasks, I muttered to myself); that a syndicate of distinguished writers would not have the impact of a single mind, whatever be its quality. The narrowness implicit in such a single-eyed view of contemporary problems could easily be corrected by other presentations, of which there is no lack. But I must declare that I have no intention of setting myself up as a *guru*. I am a senior citizen of the modern world and a senior member of the modern church. As such I have indeed reflected on most contemporary concerns. Why should I share these reflections with a wider public? Only because years of speaking and writing on the Bible have given me a familiarity with its contents and with some of what biblical scholarship old and new has produced. These reflections are presented with no dog-

matic value and nothing to recommend them except what
merits they may have.

Christians, if they are Christians, accept the supreme, even
unique importance of Jesus for the meaning of human life,
both the life of the race and the life of the individual person.
To borrow a well-worn phrase, they believe that Jesus is not
only the most important thing, he is the only thing. They believe that without him nothing else in human life and human
affairs has any significance; without him there are no values
which are not transitory. For them the usual chronology of
"before Christ" and "the year of the Lord" expresses a
truth: the life of Jesus is the central event in human history
according to which that entire history must be evaluated and
judged. They are afraid that efforts to replace this designation by "the common era" and "before the common era"
are efforts, whether deliberate and explicit or not, to impose
the non-Christian non-recognition of the centrality of Jesus
upon the common language. It may be only a question of
whose ox is gored, or who has the prior right to be offensive.
I mention this only because one's basic response to Jesus
comes up in so apparently simple a thing as B.C. and A.D.

Our problem here is to state this basic Christianity in a convincing way. I despair of even remotely imitating the recent
statement of Hans Kung on being a Christian in a book by
that title which will become a classic. Do Christians really believe what I have just stated as a basic element of Christianity? Have they not always been quick to say that this or that
element of human life is secular, that Jesus has nothing to say
to this or that problem? In fact, I shall probably say that
myself more than once before I am finished. To illustrate:
Jesus said nothing about how to drive an automobile. I have
no hesitation in asserting that there are some ways of handling this instrument which are essentially unchristian; and I
would be equally quick to say that anyone who cannot see

that does not know what being a Christian is. Let us borrow from Hans Kung and say that to be Christian is to be fully human. Do we Christians really believe that? Do I not take on an impossible task which it would be wiser to leave to another when I attempt to explode the calumny, centuries old and still alive and vigorous, that to be a Christian means to say goodbye to a full rich life, to adopt ways which are subhuman or inhuman, to renounce the entire present for an uncertain future?

Yes, it is a challenge and almost certainly a challenge which exceeds my responses. But the calumny has not been created and fostered only by unbelievers and professed enemies of Christianity. It has probably found most of its supporters among those who not only profess Christianity but think of themselves as its propagators and defenders. C.S. Lewis once made his fictitious devil say to his nephew, "Remember, when you are dealing with pleasure you are in the Enemy's (God's) territory." How many Christians have thought that all you had to do was renounce pleasure? Most, of course, professed the belief and did not live it. Others found that the pleasure of depriving others of pleasure and of managing other people's lives was more than enough to compensate for the so-called "lower" pleasures which they had renounced. They forgot or perhaps never read that Jesus was more hostile to the self-righteous than he was to prostitutes and tax-collectors—by which I do not mean that he was sympathetic to prostitution. Someone must speak to this, dangerous as it is, and I guess it falls to me.

Most of the modern concerns which we shall encounter will be called moral, or they have moral consequences. Is this forum the proper place for moral concerns to be aired? There is a science known as moral theology; its principles and practice have experienced sweeping changes in the last twenty years, which many would not hesitate to call revolutionary.

For the faithful these changes are scarcely less disturbing than the changes in the style and methods of biblical interpretation of which we have heard so much. Christian moralists do not suffer from impediments to articulate speech nor, at least in recent years, from timidity in attacking sensitive questions; I remember, as I am sure they do, some tardiness in recognizing that war, even nuclear war, is a Christian moral problem, but I think that is behind us. Should this treatment not be better (and without undue modesty be) left to those who have made Christian morality an object of professional study?

The fact that I boldy embark on this project prevents no one else, whatever be his or her professional competence, from embarking on a similar project. My own presentation may move others to share in the discussion, if for no other reason than to prove me wrong; the Christian people will be no poorer for such a decision. But this book has been entitled *Source* (not by me) for good reasons, of which one is the ancient belief that Christian morality springs from the Gospels as from a source and not from human reason nor from ethical traditions. This statement must be refined, and I shall try to do so below; but the words and the life of Jesus have a place in a specifically Christian moral teaching which is not shared with anything else. One may indeed grant that much of enlightened Christian reason and Christian moral tradition has been dedicated to finding ways of evading the words and example of Jesus, and that this still goes on; but the Christian source is still honored, even if the honor is paid more by verbal tribute to the past than by actualizing the past in the present.

Christian moral teaching has most frequently taken the form of a code of conduct, a system of "do's" and "don't's" which, when ideally complete, would cover all conceivable situations and would deliver a prefabricated answer to every moral question. Such a system, of course, is impossible, nor have Christian moral teachers tried to create it; they have worked towards it as a perpetually unfinished task. Yet this is precisely the kind of code which Jesus himself seemed to reject; it is represented by what in the New Testament is called the Law. The words of Jesus about the Law are not so unmistakably clear that they remove all dispute; scholars do claim that Jesus in some sense retained a modified understanding of the Law. Perhaps Paul misunderstood Jesus totally, but he retained no such reservation or modification; he said Christians are free from the Law. But the human instinct to codify rules of conduct—above I called it "managing other people's lives"—runs so deeply that Christians, freed from the old Law, began at once to create a new one.

Yet Christian moral teaching is not a code but an *ethos,* if I may be pardoned for using a word which I proceed at once to explain. An ethos is something every one knows and understands, even if they have never called it that. It is a way of life, a way of thinking, a way of doing (or not doing) things, associated with a group of some kind, communicated less by formal instruction than by close association with other members of the group. An ethos was communicated in a day long gone when boys and girls were taught to be ladies and gentlemen. "A lady does not do things like that" or "a gentleman does not behave that way" dealt with intangibles and unteachables; but it worked. It was not comprehensive, and it lacked some important features. A gentleman did not smoke or swear in the presence of ladies (to be carefully distinguished from women), or wear checkered clothes, or beat his slaves (but he might own them), or bully his servants, or lie, or beat his animals, or get drunk in public (only in private and with close friends), or engage in brawls (but he might engage in duels). I cannot be so explicit about ladies, but I remember hearing once of a well-known women's college whose graduates could be identified by the fact that they always wore gloves and did not cross their legs in public. I think I need only mention that tennis was once a sport played only by gentlemen to suggest that something was lost when the ideal of the gentleman was replaced by the ideal of the slob. There is an ethos of each profession, of branches of the armed services, of famous old universities, of families, and even of certain sports organizations; under Joe McCarthy the Yankees always wore neckties in dining rooms. Perhaps this helped them to beat the daylights out of everybody else in a coldly professional way. There is nothing mysterious about an ethos unless you are outside it.

It is obvious that to be a Christian is more than grudging submission to a set of rules and prohibitions, just as being a gentleman is more than the rules of proper conduct. Newman's definition of a gentleman as one who never gives pain is still valid. The ethos must rest in a set of habits which have become almost instinctive. Such a set of habits, a second nature, must be founded in a deep conviction of their importance and value and from an overpowering desire to be what the ethos proclaims one to be. One may say that such an ethos would leave very few authentic Christians, and indeed authentic Christians have always been few; but the recognition that one's Christianity is not authentic is the first step toward making it authentic. It is like learning a foreign language; one cannot speak French until one has become French. One will then make only the kind of mistakes which the French make in speaking French. With the Christian ethos, one may make wrong moral judgments, but they will be Christian mistakes.

An ethic can be framed in a set of rules. An ethos is something living; it defies codification. It must be lived and experienced; there is always something more than the formula of words can convey. It is not simply learned, it must be felt, shared, done, suffered. Who knows when the child has matured enough to carry the family traditions? Perhaps no one; but when the child has grown old enough to be one of the few carriers of those traditions, if the child, now grown to an adult, does not know and love those traditions, the traditions are no longer alive. Certainly essays such as this will not preserve the traditions alive and vigorous. It would be foolish for me to think they could; they do no more than express a reminder to my fellow Christians to know what they are.

It is evident that the Gospel as ethos must be read in a church. It is, as it was written to be, the expression of the faith of a living community. To read the Gospel as anything else but the book of a church is to read it merely as a chapter in the history of culture. This does not deny the interest and value of the study of the history of the culture; but no one is asked to venture all his life and his hope on a chapter of the history of culture now two thousand years old. The Gospel is to be read in the context of two thousand years of the Christian experience. In that experience we see how the Gospel has been lived. In that experience we may learn how to continue the Christian experience. In that experience we situate the Christian use of moral reason and the preservation of Christian moral tradition. But as the Gospel is not frozen in the text, so it is not frozen in the moral thinking and the moral traditions of the past. As living the Christian experience is critical not only of the world but of itself; for the Christian experience has never incorporated into itself the fullness of the Christian life.

The Christian experience includes dark spots as well as bright lights, and these must be recognized. Unless reflection is critical of the Christian past, it is simply a hardening of the moral arteries. Christian moral reflection must recognize that being a Christian is a perpetually unfinished job, both for the church as a whole and for individual Christians, and that

traditions long venerated may be of little or no value in forming moral judgments in new situations which were never en-
visaged when the traditions were formed; the traditions may
even be a positive moral obstacle to Christian response. A
study of the past history of Christian moral theory and practice would disclose how frequently an unthinking adherence
to established patterns of conduct deemed sacred by long-
established custom has compelled Christians to an immoral
response to situations which they refused to recognize as new.
One can hardly remove entirely the element of risk from
moral decision.

No good purpose is served, for example, by attempting to
defend the Crusades as examples of Christian zeal and
courage. It would be at least honest to recognize them as
examples of organized banditry which set European Christianity not only back to the mores of the Roman Empire, but
even beyond it. We should be willing to admit that Popes and
bishops blessed the brigands who embarked on these enterprises, and offered spiritual rewards to those who slaughtered
the unbelievers. Never was the cross so profaned. Yet our
veneration for the traditions of the past has long blinded us to
the true character of this aberration from the Gospel. It was
not only our veneration for the past, but our desire to
preserve immaculate the image of a spiritual leadership which
still survives in the successors of medieval Popes and bishops.
To admit that these earlier spiritual leaders had failed so
lamentably in their duty might open the suspicion that the
present holders of these offices are not immune from an
equally lamentable failure. Yet we are sometimes invited to
join a crusade—against smoking or obscene movies or abortion—with no awareness of what the word really means. I
would be as much flattered by an invitation to take part in a
gang rape. It would take too long to recite examples of the
times when the Crusades have been reenacted in episodes of

Christian violence, pillage and murder. So much can be drawn from one refusal of Christian tradition to criticize itself.

The Christian ethos is more than a way of life—vague as that may be. It is also a way of thinking. By this I mean the acceptance of established values and of principles upon which moral conclusions are formed. The ethos also includes a store of social experience which retains its identity in spite of constant change. It is something like a living language, to return to the example used above. This ethos of thought is identical with folk wisdom. All of us grow up with certain unreflected values and convictions. As we grow older we revise and replace them. But at any given moment, when challenged, we show what we think is really important; and we show it more honestly if the challenge is sudden and critical, allowing us no time to think about what our response ought to be. Sudden disaster, it is known, reveals an unsuspected amount of vicious selfishness in many people. What is surprising is that it also reveals resources of unsuspected heroism in so many others. No one is incapable of basic human decency—or of basic human indecency; but under pressure we shall choose one or the other according to our settled and unreflective beliefs and values.

When there is a massive disturbance of established convictions which have been long accepted by a large social group, social unrest ensues. Such seems to be the condition in large areas of the Catholic Church today. It should tell us something about the quality of Catholic faith that it is such a delicate structure that even the necessary ripping out of one thread, the necessary removal of one brick to make a patch is seen by many as a threat that the whole fabric will collapse. This is not novel; the Holy See once saw such a threat in the heliocentric theory of the solar universe. The saying of Tertullian, "Credo quia absurdum est" (I believe it because it is absurd), has become a motto of orthodoxy; absurdity alone is thought to be enough to justify faith. Over forty years ago when I presented doubts about the historical character of the exodus narrative, students asked me whether we would not at once proceed to doubt the resurrection of Jesus. I pointed out that this would be lamentably illogical. I should have said, and soon came to add, that there are dangers in thinking; there are even greater dangers in not thinking. I hope in the course of these essays to point out some of the dangers in not thinking.

I often feel that I repeat myself; perhaps my readers will tell me that I do not have this feeling often enough. Nevertheless, I am compelled to say once more that the Christian act of faith is a personal experience which must be lived anew by each Christian each day in a constantly changing situation in life. It is not something which can be done once and then forgotten; it is not something we need not do for ourselves because some one else has done it. It is not an experience which, once had in childhood, remains valid for the rest of one's life. For many of us, faith is a childhood experience which has never been revoked. It retains the inexperience and immaturity of childhood because it has never become an adult experience. It is our security blanket which recalls those early days in which we could always count on some adult to intervene when crisis developed.

The crisis of adult life is the awareness that we are responsible. In most of the areas of human experience we rejoice in the freedom and responsiblility of adulthood. In religion we still look for someone to tell us what to do and preserve our happy freedom of irresponsibility; we seem to be afraid to grow up. We need not develop our own Christian principles and convictions; there are spiritual leaders who tell us, or who ought to tell us what those Christian principles and convictions are. The convictions need not enter our soul; we can wear them like a garment. We need not be troubled by moral decisions; our spiritual leaders will tell us what moral decisions to make, and we can trust them because they are infallible. These are the same infallible teachers who blessed the Crusades. Does the church in the last analysis satisfy us because it liberates us from the responsibility of moral decision?

I speak with some urgency about the security blanket because I perceive this desire for false security as a major threat to Christian integrity. I do not suggest that I see everything; others may see other needs equally or more urgent. I trust them to address these needs. Let me say that we shall all agree that the Christian can find no other security except the church, which is the living Christ. The church is also, as the church has said of herself, the pilgrim people on the road to fulfillment. This fulfillment she has not yet achieved. She will attain that fulfillment only by constantly reaffirming and redefining her identity with Jesus. When she fails to reaffirm and redefine, the identity is dimmed.

CHAPTER ONE

DEATH

ONE'S view of death is certainly affected by the passage of time. Some years ago I was aware of death only as something which happened to other people, most frequently to the old, rarely and by tragic exception to the young. It was not something which entered realistically into any plans I might make. Now I face the fact that death is an experience which most of my contemporaries have had. It will happen to me before it happens to most of the people I meet if they take no more than reasonable care of themselves. I can no longer put it out of my mind as something which I need not think about. And I now realize that I may not really believe in life after death (more on this in Chapter Eight). I am not trying to share this problem with anyone else. Perhaps I do the world no good by saying that the simple faith in eternal life which I suppose I once had is not as simple or as easy as it was when death did not seem to be a near and real threat. Samuel Johnson once said that the prospect of being hanged concentrates a man's mind wonderfully. My observation has been that this prospect, or something like it—a sentence of death from a doctor, for example—often shatters the mind, destroys what appeared to be perfect calm and peace of soul, and reduces apparently strong men and women to hysterical tears. It is a doubtful advantage that man is the only animal which knows it is going to die. There are, however, other responses. The legendary Marine sergeant of Chateau-Thierry addressed his squad with an epithet as he led them over the top, "Come on, you _____, do you want to live forever?" It is hard to tell how anyone will respond to the last great crisis as they realize that it is really the first when they have never given it much thought.

16

Much has been written about death, none of it from first-hand experience. It is a theme in some of the earliest literature we know, the literature from the ancient Near East, two and perhaps three thousand years before Christ. A brief consideration of some of these pieces will suggest that nothing very new has been said about death since these earliest reflections. In ancient Mesopotamia the myth of Adapa appeared in writing over two thousand years B.C. It tells of a man who was offered immortality by a god but was deprived of it by the deception of another god. In the myth of Gilgamesh the hero finds, after a long and dangerous search, the plant of immortality, but it is stolen from him by a snake before he has a chance to eat it. A goddess whom he encounters during the search warns him: "The life you seek you will not find. The gods have given death to man as his portion, but have reserved life for themselves. Enjoy the simple pleasures of life as long as you can." Her warning is echoed almost verbally in the saying of a biblical wise man at least two thousand years later: "Go, eat your bread with joy and drink your wine with a merry heart, because it is now that God favors your works. At all times let your garments be white, and spare not the perfume from your head. Enjoy life with the wife whom you love, all the days of the fleeting life that is granted you under the sun. This is your lot in life, for the toil of your labors under the sun. Anything you can turn your hand to, do with what power you have; for there will be no work, nor reason, nor knowledge, nor wisdom in the nether world where you are going" (Ecclesiastes 9:7-10). This is not all we find in the Old Testament about death; but it should be noticed that this wise man speaks with the majority of the ancient world.

What is expressed in these passages is a profound pessimism before death; death is the ultimate negative to everything human, every desire, every ambition, every achievement, every hope which life offers. This pessimism is

joined with a candid hedonism which, carried to its logical
conclusion, would affirm that a pleasure postponed could
easily be a pleasure renounced forever; and what good would
that do? There is a certain charming inconsistency in human
behavior which preserves a basic human decency even against
the ruthless logic of hedonism; perhaps this basic human
decency is as much a mystery as death, which it scorns and
mocks. This will have to be discussed under another heading.

The ancient Egyptians followed their own way in this as in
other questions of life. Ancient Egyptian art has told us more
about the daily life, manners, dress, housing, work and play
of the ancient Egyptians than we know about any other
ancient people. All this art was found in tombs. The tomb
paintings represent a two-dimensional world into which one
passed at death. The Egyptian found life under the warm sun
of the Nile valley so satisfactory that he dreamed of nothing
better than a continuation of the same life after death. And as
no moral condition was imposed upon entrance into the present life, so there was none imposed upon entrance into the
next life. "The Book of the Dead" is a compilation of the
correct answers to be given when one was challenged on entrance into the next world; to be sure that the deceased might
not stumble in his responses, a copy of the correct answers
was buried with him. It was not death the Egyptians feared,
but, like the Greeks, decay and corruption. Eternal life could
not be assured unless the body were decently interred and, at
least for kings and nobles, mummified and placed in a tomb
suitable to the dignity of the deceased; but even the Egyptians
found the luxury of a monumental pyramid too rich for their
tastes. Ancient Egyptians did not so much affirm life after
death as deny the reality of death, more subtly and less crass-
ly than that reality is denied in such places as Forest Lawn.

Yet even the conventional orthodoxy of ancient Egypt,
which endured for twenty-five hundred years, broke down

under stress—the belief that the present life is so good that one can hope for nothing better than to continue political and social stability. For most of its history Egypt enjoyed such stability, matching the stability of its climate, which includes none of the terrors of nature such as storms, high winds, earthquakes or volcanic eruptions. In Egypt it does not even rain; the Nile furnishes all the water that is needed. But there were periods of political and social unrest, and sometime early in the second millennium B.C. two writings appeared which have been preserved. The Song of the Harper candidly does not believe in the Egyptian mythology of death. The singer recommends that one seek and embrace all the pleasure available, because there is nothing to hope for after death. This theme we have already seen, and we recognized it as one of the standard human approaches to death. The Dialogue of a Man with his Soul presents reasons why suicide is the only rational response when life has become total defeat and frustration. The soul argues against this; and in fact as far as we know suicide was not a usual Egyptian response to the difficulty of living. The man sees death as release and repose; it is rest after toil, recovery after disease, return from exile, release from prison, a cool breeze on a hot day, food and drink after fasting. The dialogue is not complete and we do not know how the dispute was resolved; but the writer has given all the arguments to the man, and leaves the soul nothing but conventional beliefs which do not correspond to reality.

As far as I know, and I do not claim to have read everything, this is the first instance in literature of the proposition that death is not the riddle which makes nonsense out of life but the solution to the problems of life. When life becomes intolerable, death must be sought and embraced. Centuries after the dialogue the Stoic philosophers recommended that life should be voluntarily terminated when it is no longer possible to sustain it with pleasure and dignity. There is an almost contemporary note in this appeal to what is now called the quality of life, which alone is thought to make life worth preserving. One observes that neither in the ancient nor in the modern world has this appeal to death as the ultimate solution of all human problems been attractive to the majority of mankind.

In the classical literature of ancient Greece and Rome, which formed so much of the thinking of western civilization, death appears often, and, except for the Stoic eccentricity noted above, always as the enemy who is the last victor in all battles. A fragment of the tragedies of Euripides asks, "Who knows whether to live is to die, and to die is to live?" The profound pessimism which overclouded Greece and Rome in the presence of death was even stronger than the hedonism which was, it turns out, not a sure escape from the terror of death. I ask forgiveness for quoting the Latin of some celebrated lines of the Roman poet Catullus, a contemporary of Julius Caesar: "Soles occidere et redire possunt;/ Nobis, cum semel occidit brevis lux,/ Nox est perpetua una dormienda," which may be rendered: The sun sets and returns again; but for us, once our brief light has set, there is nothing but one eternal night of sleep." Catullus, certainly a hedonist if there ever was one, addressed these lines to his mistress, a Roman lady of quality whom he masks as Lesbia; hardly any other woman has ever elicited a body of such delicately executed verse. The thought of that eternal night is used to urge Lesbia to yield to the pleasures of love. Another Roman, Horace, thought that he overcame death by the creation of immortal verse, which he described as a monument more lasting than bronze. Many have taken comfort in their achievements, which will outlive them. I have thought of this when I read that the ruins of modern civilization, unlike the ruins of ancient Egypt, Greece and Rome, are most likely to be the remains of grain elevators, bridges and the like.

The ancients knew the rationalization which finds that death for a good cause is worthwhile. The same Horace wrote that it is pleasant and beautiful to die for one's country. Most commentators have remarked that given the chance to do this pleasant and beautiful thing, he did not do it. It must be conceded that the expiring Roman Republic hardly presented itself as a pleasant and beautiful cause. The rationalization, which is perhaps the most attractive of all the futile rationalizations of death, breaks down if one is asked to state a cause which is not itself subject to the universal curse of mortality. Yet one of the most attractive traits of the human psyche is its ability to make the irrational judgment that there are things bigger than itself; and certainly man looks better facing death in this way than he does whimpering at the approach of Catullus's eternal night. But then one must admit that many, if not most, are spurious, and those which are not spurious are only temporary achievements. Why should one die for posterity when posterity itself must also die, when posterity does not seem likely to be any better than we are?

We turn now to the biblical view of death, remarking first that there is no biblical view of death. The books of the Old Testament with a few exceptions exhibit all the views which we have noticed elsewhere in the ancient world. These few exceptions are late books from the last two or three centuries before the Christian era in which belief in the resurrection of the dead appears. This will be discussed below at greater length; we omit it here because it is simply not an Old Testament belief. In most of the Old Testament books death is accepted as an inescapable reality, not unnatural unless it is premature; and even premature death, in a world in which infant mortality, disease and starvation were threats which they are not in the modern western world, was hardly unnatural in the sense that it was rare and unexpected. The ancient

Israelite expected to die and accepted the prospect; he hoped that death would not come too soon or too slowly. When it came, he would be joined to his fathers; he would pass from the community of the living to the community of the dead. I read some years ago that only recently has the number of the living come to exceed the number of the dead. The source did not tell us how that calculation was reached.

There are Old Testament voices which do not express resignation. The author of the book of Job, whose identity and date are unknown, was not the typical Israelite any more than Plato was a typical Athenian. There may have been others before him who anticipated the major confrontation with death which occurs in the book. He attacks the mystery of death from every angle, and in the end is baffled. It is only in bitter irony that he presents death as rest and release, the same theme expressed in the Egyptians dialogue of the man with his soul:

> There the wicked cease from troubling,/there the weary are at rest.
> There the captives are at ease together,/and hear not the voice of the slave driver.
> Small and great are the same,/and the servant is free from his master (3:17-18).

The writer expresses the idea that life is so bad that death is an improvement. But nobody seriously believes this, and the idea was not shared by another wise man equally pessimistic, Koheleth: "A live dog is better off than a dead lion" (Ecclesiastes 9:4). And he thus answers the continuation of Job's complaint:

> Why is light given to the toilers,/ and life to the bitter of spirit?

> They wait for death and it comes not;/they search for it rather
> than for hidden treasures (3:20-21).

Indeed one may ask now as the ancient Egyptian poet did whether this is not the attitude of the suicide; I can plead only that suicide has never been regarded as a normal response even to overwhelming troubles, and that it is impossible to enter into the feelings of the suicide unless you have shared the experience.

In a line which anticipates Catullus's line quoted above, Job reflects on the irreversibility of death:

> For a tree there is hope,/ if it be cut down, that it will sprout
> again,/ and that its tender shoots will not cease.
> Even though its root grow old in the earth,/ and its stump die
> in the dust.
> Yet at the first whiff of water it may flourish again/ and put
> forth branches like a young plant.
> But when a man dies, all vigor leaves him;/ when man ex-
> pires, where is he (14:7-9)?

Certainly the author of these words did not expect the resurrection which Jerome, by some skillful manipulation of a corrupt and unintelligible Hebrew text, found in a later passage of the book (19:25-27). Although Job's reflections upon death follow a serpentine course, it never occurs to him to think of death as anything but final, terminal, irreversible.

The friends of Job express the traditional wisdom that swift and painful death happens only to sinners, and that the righteous enjoy a long life and an easy death. Job confutes this with the statement that the righteous are just as dead as the wicked—apart from the fact that experience does not support this allotment of death according to merits.

One dies in his full vigor,/ wholly at ease and content;
His figure is full and nourished,/ and his bones are rich in marrow.
Another dies in bitterness of soul,/ never having tasted happiness.
Alike they lie down in the dust,/ and worms cover them both (21:23-26).

Job does not seem aware of the myth of Eden (Genesis 2-3), which is a kind of response to traditional wisdom. Since death is universal, and since there is no visible apportionment of sudden, premature or painful death according to merits, it can only be explained by the fact that human wickedness, as universal as death, is the cause of death. This does not explain the death of infants; and this comes from the fact that they are members of a guilty race, guilty with an ancestral guilt which goes back to the very first human ancestors. The myth has often but not successfully been traced to roots in other ancient Near Eastern mythology; it remains unique. Other myths like the Mesopotamian myth of Adapa attribute human mortality to the jealousy of the gods or of some god, who were unwilling to see man share the divine prerogative of immortality. This theme is at least not as obvious in the myth of Eden as it is in other ancient myths, although the myth of Eden was never intended to carry all the weight which Paul, Augustine and the Council of Trent laid upon it. It is somewhat strange that there is no clear allusion to the myth of Eden elsewhere in the Hebrew Bible, which nowhere links death to universal or hereditary guilt.

Paul in his Epistle to the Romans (5) formulates an antithesis between Adam, the founder of the race, the author of sin and death, and Jesus Christ, the founder of a new race and the author of grace and life. The death of Jesus has paradoxically become the work of life, the source of the new life of grace for all mankind as the sin of Adam has been the source of death for all mankind. Jesus has overcome death by rising and overcome sin by not sinning. The two great enemies of mankind, sin and death, must be vanquished together. This exposition is found in the Epistle to the Romans, the last of the writings of Paul, and it was probably brought together for the first time in this Epistle, although its elements are found in the earlier Epistles. The death and resurrection of Jesus Christ and the hope of rising in union with him are the Christian response to the riddle, the mystery, the enigma, the irrationality of death.

In the first Epistle to the Corinthians, which is among the earliest of the writings of Paul, he states emphatically at length that the resurrection of Jesus is the assurance of eternal life. Jesus has overcome death by rising from the dead— although, to speak precisely in the language of Paul, it is God who raises him from the dead. Later developments in Christology make it somewhat difficult for us to use the language of Paul without further refinement. But to speak of the resurrection is only the first step. Christian faith in the resurrection is not simply a restatement of the Pharisaic belief in the resurrection. Paul is insistent that both Christ and the believer rise to a new life and not to a resumption of the life which is terminated by death. To the Christians whom Paul addressed, who were mostly the destitute, harried by disease and physical weakness, oppressed by the powerful and by the government, often enslaved, whose days were consumed in toil or in hopeless idleness, a resumption of life would not offer much, and Christian belief would not allow them to think of Lazarus the beggar rising to the life of Dives the rich man. Paul found it impossible to describe the new life which Jesus promised, but he did his best—perhaps occasionally overstating his case. Without the insights available to Paul, I shall not run the same risk, except to say that those who think that the resurrection is pie in the sky when you die manifest less their own unbelief than their simple ignorance of the world of discourse of the New Testament.

Jesus has given death a redeeming value which it never had. This does not mean that heroic death for others was unknown to the ancient world; as we noticed above, this is one of the nobler ways in which men have looked at death, even if it is ultimately irrational. Perhaps one's mind is closed to certain values unless one becomes a bit irrational—love, for instance. But only the death of Jesus is presented as not merely saving the life which one has—a postponement of death—but as opening the possibilities of a new life. Christians are invited to unite themselves with Jesus in his life and death and thus to give their own life and death a redeeming value. This is not presented as a reasonable alternative to the supreme irrationality of death, which Catullus sugar-coated by the prospect of a thousand kisses. Jesus does offer the hope of human fulfillment. Those who think Catullus was right may console themselves with the thought of how much lechery has done for mankind—and womankind, too.

The victory of Jesus over death should not be separated from his victory over sin. In Christ it has been proved that one man could live without sin. A somewhat defective Christology has left many believers thinking that sin for Jesus was impossible and that he did not sin for some other reason than that he chose not to sin. They have therefore decided that his victory over sin could not be shared by them. If Jesus did not make it possible for each human being to live without the assistance, the consolations and the pleasure which are derived from sin and thus to escape death, he did nothing for us. Rudolph Bultmann once wrote that Jesus alone realized the full possibilities of human existence.

I have reviewed, I think, most of the approaches to death which men have adopted since they first began to think about it, and this is a long time. Nothing except the Christian approach is a response to the appalling waste of human life, and the threat of nothingness which looms so near to all of us. Plato said of his own hope of immortality, "It is an attractive risk and a great hope." I cannot prove that the Christian hope is justified. But my review will be incomplete unless I look at the most recent rationalization, produced in our own generation, a generation which has seen men, women and children die like fruit flies. For most citizens of the modern world, their deaths are about as meaningful as the death of the fruit fly. Ivan Illich, one of the keener observers and more incisive critics of the modern world, has written: "Death that was once viewed as a call from God, and later as a natural event, has become an untimely event that is the outcome of our technical failure to treat a disease." Illich has certainly pinned down the contemporary belief or hope—shall I call it a delusion?—that death is simply the last disease which has not surrendered to medicine. I expect to be railed at as hopelessly out of touch with contemporary science if I think that because people have always died, they always will. Modern medicine deals with reality; Christian theology and preaching can be in skilled hands beautiful, but do they not deal with unreality?

Let us take Illich's saying as a basis for some reflection. He is a phrasemaker, as I think I am, and we sometimes cut corners too sharply when we turn a phrase. Illich knows, and I suppose those who think he describes it know that medicine will not cope with all forms of death. I have read that the major cause of death among young white male adults under thirty in the United States is the automobile accident, and the major cause of death among young black male adults of the same age group is murder. Are these failures of medicine or of medical technology? Last year several thousand people died prematurely in Northern Ireland; would more doctors and hospitals have saved their lives? Between 1939 and 1945 millions of people died prematurely in Europe and Asia; percentagewise there were probably fewer who died in the Black Death in 1347 and 1348, but this enormous attack on human life did not come from a virus or a bacillus. In recent years millions of people have died of starvation. People have been starving to death for thousands of years; but never before have so many starved to death when the production, storage and transporation of food were so marvelously advanced. It was not lack of medical facilities which let these millions die; nor was it a failure of the production and distribution of food. If we continue to work on medicine and medical techniques—not without reason is it called the health industry—we may reach the point when no one will die except by violence. May I timidly submit the suggestion that this will do the job so long and so thoroughly done by epidemic disease? If it happens, must we say to the doctors, "Canst thou but minister to a mind diseased?"

Am I not dealing in absurdities and refusing to take seriously some very serious problems? I wish to state as emphatically as I can that I am deadly serious. Why should I think that something will happen to correct the belief that violence, death-dealing violence, is the quick and easy solution to most modern problems except those of health? I may have misunderstood Jesus when I interpret him as saying that if men did not sin they would not die; but the propositon is no more absurd than the belief that man has no problems which cannot be medicaly handled, and a refusal to admit that the basic human problem is man's will for evil. The greatest threat to human life has always been other people.

Chapter Two

MARRIAGE

AN old and dear friend of mine, now dead a few years, taught the treatise on matrimony in a seminary for most of his active life. We used to discuss regularly a problem which he had written about in his dissertation, and which he confessed candidly that he had trouble teaching; and I may say that my friend was possessed of possibly the keenest mind I have met in now seventy-one years of experience. The problem which exercised him was the theological thesis which asserts the exclusive jurisdiction of the church over sacramental marriage. He felt that he really had no proof of this thesis; and since he was afflicted with a rare honesty which can create problems for a theologian, he felt ill at ease in presenting it.

And well he might. The claim of exclusive jurisdiction over sacramental marriage is a corollary of the sacramental character of marriage. Marriage has been enumerated as the seventh of the sacraments for centuries; to be exact we have no evidence that this enumeration is any earlier than the tenth century. When we ask what Jesus said or is alleged to have said about the sacrament of marriage, or what the New Testament says, we draw a blank. This does not mean that the New Testament says nothing about marriage; it says something— very little, in comparison to the large place which marriage has in the doctrinal and pastoral instruction of the modern Church. I mean that the New Testament is unaware that marriage is a sacrament. The old translation, "This is a great sacrament" (Ephesians 5:12), came from a misunderstanding of the Greek word *mysterion* (no longer translated "sacrament" in the New American Bible), and explicity referred not to marriage but to Christ and the church in the text.

If we turn to the Old Testament, we find a pattern of marriage which the Church has never made her own, although with the exception of divorce (to which we shall devote a separate essay), it is nowhere repudiated in the New Testament. Paul makes the polygamous marriages of Abraham a type of the dealings of God with the Jews and the Gentiles (Galatians 4:21-31). This is hardly equivalent to a repudiation of the practice. Jeremiah wrote a parable in which Israel and Judah are the wives of Yahweh, and Ezekiel used the same parable twice. The Old Testament shows no awareness of any religious character of marriage. The evidence about Israelite and Jewish marriage, scanty as it is, does not exhibit any religious attitude towards marriage different from the attitude in Mesopotamia, Canaan or other ancient Near Eastern countries.

It might therefore seem that marriage is a topic which does not allow much room for theological discourse; and while no doubt it has theological implications and is an issue such as I described in my opening essay in this book, it is an issue loaded with traps for the unwary, and even for the wary. The trap which I have mostly in mind is illustrated by an anecdote, surely quite ancient and well worn, about an elderly matron who had just heard the Monsignor preach a sermon about marriage. Asked about her response, she said. "Ah, praise God, it was beautiful, and I wish I knew as little about the subject as himself does." We Catholics do suffer from a plethora of books, articles, counseling and so forth about marriage produced by a celibate clergy. To say that their detachment equips them to deal with a subject which often arouses passion suggests that tone-deafness gives one an edge in musical criticism, or color-blindness an advantage in art criticism. Frankly, I have never found a good answer to Catholics who ask why priests, if they are not going to marry, insist on talking about it so much. Marriage is a basic and almost universal human experience from which we priests for alleged good reasons have deliberately excluded ourselves. I write this essay on request with a clear knowledge, which I ask my readers to share, that it lacks the intimate understanding which experience alone gives.

But the experience of mankind is wider, although not deeper, than the experience of a single person or of a single group; and this is all I wish to point out. Cultural narrowness, in which ignorance and prejudice are rooted, is as old and wide as mankind itself. Human groups live in their own little world, convinced that their own way of doing things is not only the best way, it is the only right way; and when they discover massive deviations from their own way, they regard them as subhuman, or even as contrary to human nature. The traditional Catholic theology of marriage implied a belief in the unity and stability of human nature; and the human nature which theology knew was the human nature of western Europe, Christendom. Thus when Europeans learned that there were vast previously unknown continents full of people, they believed that they should make these people Christian, and at once assumed that this meant to make them European. But they could not make them European landlords, nobles, merchants or scholars; they could only turn them into peasants or unskilled laborers, hewers of wood and drawers of water in the temple of European culture. Often this meant enslaving them; but this was esteemed as liberation from slavery to the devil. This may seem a long way around the barn to my subject; but it meant imposing European patterns of marriage upon the natives. It took a few hundred years even for scholars to learn that the social patterns of marriage are cultural rather than religious; some do not know it yet.

Permit me to tell an anecdote of how the character of European Christian imperialism became clear to me for the first time in my life. In 1970 I was invited to a lecture tour in Tanzania, Uganda and Kenya. It became clear to me that one of the major obstacles to evangelization in East Africa had long been the practice of polygamy. Missionaries had for decades insisted on the natural law of monogamy and required converts to renounce all wives except the first. There is no place in the culture of East Africa for the unattached woman, especially if she has children. Hence the dismissed wives were usually compelled into the stews of Dar-es-Salaam and Nairobi in order to survive. This did not bother the missionaries; after all prostitution is a Christian vice, found in Rome, Paris and London. But polygamy is against the natural law, and the women who were forced into brothels were actually, the Europeans thought, being raised to a high level of civilization and morality. No thought was given to the fact that polygamy provided a decent status and often happiness for a surplus of women, and no effort was made to find a substitute. Churchmen bleated about the "sanctity of marriage" (which they could not prove) and thought they had done their duty. Father Eugene Hillman, who gave serious constructive thought to this problem of evangelization, was simply reassigned out of Africa after he published some of his ideas.

Yet what has monogamy to do with Christianity? Monogamy was practiced by the Greeks and Romans before the Christian era. The polygamy of the patriarchs and of other Old Testament heroes (or those esteemed as heroes) was an embarrassment to the church from early times (not to Paul, as we have noticed); and the church Fathers dealt with the embarrassment by asserting a quite unattested dispensation from the natural law for these men. A dispensation had to be postulated; they were holy men (not so clear to us now), and a genuinely holy man cannot be ignorant of the precepts of the natural law, even the secondary precepts (monogamy could not be a primary precept, or it would not be dispensable). So much was necessary to make it possible to impose the dominant cultural pattern of western Europe upon humanity. Yet polygamy serves its purpose at least as well as Christian marriage, which is rarely ideal in purpose and execution. In modern times this is not to say much for either.

It seems (and here I risk an opinion which I should perhaps suppress) that both monogamy and polygamy, if they are to fulfill their social and personal purposes, demand a high degree of dedication which is not always present. It is true that the union can survive even the lack of dedication of one of the parties, but in modern times one is not expected to pick up for the other. When marriages fail, whether polygamous or monogamous, it is a failure of people, not of institutions. It may be surprising that I mention dedication in such an obviously male-dominated institution as polygamy. But even a male-dominated institution cannot succeed without some personal dedication.

In the recent western world the idea of dedication has been replaced by the idea of romantic love as the key to marraige. The theme of most modern novels, dramas and short stories is romantic love. Most people do not realize how modern this idea is. In the Middle Ages and down to the modern period romantic love was found only outside of marriage. One is tempted to say that in contemporary society that is still the case, except that now it is not found outside of marriage, it is a substitute for it. In the ancient and medieval worlds as well as in the western world up to the twentieth century marriage was too important to be left to what were thought to be the whims of young people. Marriage was an affair with great social implications, and the selection of spouses was not left to adolescents; it was a determination reached by the mutual agreement of families. Whether the young people loved each other was not important. Married love was thought to be one of those adult skills which are learned with mature years. If the parties did not learn it, it was recognized that it was not necessary. Social pressure held unloving couples together. Did it produce unhappiness? It most certainly did; unloving marriages provided grist for the mill of novelists and dramatists. I am not maintaining the thesis that Christian marriage has ever been a remarkably successful institution. As I said above, it requires a certain amount of dedication which has not always been present. It is worth our notice that romantic love does not supply the missing dedication.

Should marriage ever have been the altar on which young people were sacrificed for family wealth and prestige? Probably not, and the modern western world has decided for several generations that it should not be. Yet one hesitates; hence the "probably." One is not sure that the social and personal consequences of what amounts to legalized promiscuity are any more desirable. The evidence, I suppose, is not in. To me—again to an inexperienced observer—this seems like saying the evidence is not in that the *Titanic* has a hole in its hull. After all, the officers might have said—but they did not—that the *Titanic* was unsinkable. And is not western civilization, the noblest of man's works, unsinkable?

Were it not for one book, one would say that the Old Testament does not know romantic love; it exhibits a patriarchal polygamous male-centered society. The one book is the Song of Songs, or the Song of Solomon. It is a short book and I recommend it in a modern translation for mature readers. It is so candid an expression of romantic love that ancient Jewish and Christian interpreters felt compelled to treat it as an allegory of divine love. The Fifth Ecumenical Council condemned Theodore of Mopsuestia because, among other alleged errors, he said the Song of Songs is a love poem. He was almost right; it is a collection of love poems, with no suggestion that any allegory is intended. It is not even clear that the lovers in the poems are married. My friend and colleague, Marvin Pope of Yale, in his recent Anchor Bible volume has pointed out dozens of passages in which the Song is more explicit sexually than interpreters have previously recognized. If Paul (or the author of Ephesians) could make the love of man and woman an image of the love of Christ and the church, he can hardly have thought it was something nasty. It is not my intention to state that romantic love (of which by office and state I have no experience) has no place in marriage, or that it does not contribute to the happiness of marriage; I merely wish to point out that it can exist without marriage, and that marriage has existed without romantic love more often than with it.

This leads me into the traditional Catholic teaching about the primary end of marriage, only recently modified. The primary end of marriage was taught to be, in the quaint Latinate phraseology of moral theology, the procreation and the education of children. Nothing but the desire to get children and to rear them was a justification for the sexual union of the parties. A secondary end—important but secondary—was "the mutual assistance" rendered by the spouses to each other. Thus theology paid a grudging recognition of the fact that human sexual love might be one of the comforts of life. In the late 1930s, Dr. Herbert Doms proposed the personalist understanding of marriage which suggested that the traditional secondary aim was as important as the traditional primary aim. Doms escaped somehow an explicit condemnation from Rome. Theologians faithfully did their duty as loyal servants of the Holy See, and the personalist theory seemed to die an ignoble death. It rose to new life with the Second Vatican Council, which recognized that in marriage people are of primary importance.

Even before the Second Vatican Council I used to call the traditional teaching the breeding-pen theory of marriage. I see no reason for withdrawing from this irreverence now. Perhaps no good is served by thrashing a dead horse; we are striving for an understanding of marriage which shows greater esteem than a theory which equates the spouses with studs and dams. We may not be succeeding. But we have to admire the countless husbands and wives who made a go of their Christian marriage in spite of the fact that their church not only gave them no help but rather added to their burdens, and constantly traduced their state of life as inferior, in which they were assimilated to barnyard animals. The church threw these moral weaklings a sop which was called "the remedy of concupiscence." No, there is probably no use in going over old wounds. But there is room for some sackcloth and ashes on us clergy for our failure to respect, honor and lead married people for so many years, and for our binding heavy burdens upon them which we did not move a finger to lift. And all this was done to preserve a theory of the ends of marriage for which there is not a shred of theological evidence.

The book of Proverbs closes with the alphabetic acrostic of the good wife (31:10-31). I suspect that modern feminists do not like this tribute to their sex. It is quite clear that the good wife is a good housekeeper before anything else. She is a good manager and a tremendously hard worker: in a world in which the working day extended from sunrise to sunset, she is praised for going beyond those hours. The Palestinian housewife awakened the household and put the household to bed. For these services her husband praises her and is proud of her. She is not admired as a career woman, and career women were not unknown in those days. Mesopotamian business records from the second millennium B.C. and Jewish papyri from the fifth century B.C. in Egypt reveal the names of some women—not many, but how many are there now?—who appear to have been active and successful in the business world of their day. Whether the scribe knew and implicitly rejected the idea of such careers is not clear; what he proposes is an ideal within the reach of any Palestinian housewife—of means, I must add; his good wife is married to a substantial citizen. There are limitations to his ideal. I said above that men and women have always identified the ideals of marriage with the cultural patterns in which we live. The Israelite scribe did this; we, perhaps without realizing it, do it also. To reject the ideal of the housewife is to say that most women have devoted their lives to degrading tasks and to fault them for not having been geniuses enough to see it. There have not been many mute inglorious village Miltons male or female. The village Cromwells have more frequently found fulfillment. After all, that takes less talent.

I did not mean to dismiss Ephesians 5:22-23 as of little consequence just because of a historic mistranslation of the Greek word *mysterion,* "mystery," as *sacramentum,* "sacrament." In fact the passage contains the longest statement about marriage in the New Testament; and while it is probably not the work of Paul but of an associate, no one doubts that it comes from apostolic tradition. It deserves close study as a witness of early Christian thinking about what marriage between Christians should be, a question on which no words attributed to Jesus himself are preserved. It would be idle to deny that the passage raises certain problems for many modern readers, and I shall have to face these problems. Let us say in the first place that a marriage in which a man loves his wife as Christ loves the church is not sick. The writer does not mean to imply that a man gives his wife everything, even reality, as Christ gives reality to the church. He means that a man should show his wife that kind of total devotion which Christ gave to the church, living and dying for it and becoming one with it. The writer evokes Genesis 2:24 to illustrate the unity of Christ and the church. It was written of a Jesuit father of some minor fame years ago that he was the only man who ever loved his neighbor with the same fierce love with which other men love themselves. This fierce love is what the writer says a man should have for his wife.

So far, the modern reader might say, so good; no woman could ask for more, and many would wonder whether she could ask as much. So why does the writer spoil everything by saying that the wife should submit to her husband as the church submits to Christ, that it is her duty to show respect as it is her husband's duty to show love? Why does he not say simply that she should love her husband as she loves herself? Many modern women will not accept the writer's analogy that the husband is head of his wife as Christ is head of his body the church. I am not about to say that they should. The men I know hardly fit the analogy of Christ the head of the church, and some fail to fit it lamentably, even tragically. We shall not serve the cause of truth by pretending that the unrealities are real. But it should be noticed that the love of husband for wife which the writer proposes was as great a departure from his cultural patterns as it is from ours; and we should not lose sight of it in pursuit of another cultural pattern.

I have spoken more than once of imposing cultural patterns upon marriage as if they were inflexible laws of human nature. The writer of Ephesians, bound by his own cultural limitations, was simply incapable of grasping a cultural pattern in which the duty of the woman would not be submission and obedience. Let us not, with a cultural shortsightedness which matches his own, insist that nothing but a pattern of equality makes happy marriage possible, and that where this pattern has been missing marriages have never been happy. May I modestly suggest that this is like denying the possibility that the Masai can be good Christians because they are not like us, civilized? Some breadth of vision which admits that there are other ways of doing things besides ours is essential for the cohabitation of different races, peoples and religions. We need not admit that other ways are as good as ours, or that we should adopt them; we should admit their right to exist. One may say that this would lead to a world without principles; but somehow I do not think that this is a very real threat. It is my plea for mutual tolerance and understanding that is unrealistic, if anything is. As one who undertook some reflection on human problems as related to biblical theology, what other plea can I enter?

The experience of some thousands of years seems to show that there is no certainly right way for the human community to institute marriage, and no way which is so bad that nothing can be made of it. Like other social systems, it is no better than the people in it. It returns no more than people put into it. It seems to me, a detached observer, that marriage in any social system requires a high degree of mutual dedication which not enough people are willing to give. This I have already said; perhaps a detached observer can say no more, and risks saying too much by saying that. One would think that one's marriage deserves as much attention, planning, care and sacrifice as the maintenance of one's car or one's house. One reads the newspapers and one wonders how many people believe it. It is easier to get a new spouse than it is to get a new car or a new house.

Chapter Three

DIVORCE

A few years ago I published an article in which I adopted a suggestion of the late Joseph Bonsirven about the interpretation of Matthew 5:32 and Matthew 19:9. These verses contain the exception "for adultery" added to the prohibition of divorce which Matthew has in common with Mark 10:11-12 and Luke 16:18. Bonsirven suggested that the exception in Matthew is apparent rather than real. The word which is translated "adultery" usually does not mean adultery, and in the context of Matthew most probably refers to marriages prohibited under the levitical degrees of kinship. Thus Matthew is to be understood as Mark and Luke are, and the words express an absolute prohibition of divorce.

This was not the only point nor even the major point I made in the article; but it was picked up by a colleague who noticed only that McKenzie supported the absolute prohibition of divorce affirmed in Church law. One wishes that colleagues who wish to quote one's writings would take the trouble to read the entire piece which they quote; it was not very long, nor did I think it was unusually dense—for exegetical discourse, anyway. But I am happy that this book affords me an opportunity to state at greater length and I hope with greater clarity the two points which I made in the earlier article. These points are: 1. the words of Jesus—and here most interpreters believe we hear his words—prohibit divorce without qualification; 2. church law is less than faithful to the teaching of Jesus by maintaining this absolute prohibition.

To the first point: The late Vincent Taylor, in his commentary on Mark published thirty years ago and since become a classic, said there is no doubt that the text of Mark on divorce

40

presents very nearly the words of Jesus, and that with all reverence we depart from his words. There is a certain refreshing honesty about this statement. It manifests that fidelity to the text which is the first duty of the interpreter; and it says frankly that we are not going to follow it without passing through semantic stunts and contortions which permit us to argue that the text really says what we want it to say. The background of the saying of Jesus is worth repeating. Everywhere except in Matthew 5:32 it is a response to a question about the grounds of divorce. On this question the rabbis were divided into those of the school of Hillel, who interpreted the grounds liberally, and Shammai, who interpreted them strictly. The dispute centered upon Deuteronomy 24:1, the only text of the Old Testament which suggests any grounds for divorce; and the grounds are there said to be something indecent (New American Bible), surely as vague as any one could wish. Shammai understood the indecency to be adultery and nothing less. Hillel understood it to be anything displeasing, or even less pleasing to the husband; examples were that he did not like her cooking, or that he found another woman who pleased him better. When Jesus was asked on which side he stood in this dispute, he said neither. The argument supposes that men and only men can divorce; I am not yet convinced by the arguments presented by my colleague and neighbor Bernadette Brooten that some rabbis accepted the possibility that wives might divorce their husbands, as they could in Roman law.

Until I am so convinced, I find no indication that Jesus spoke to a situation in Roman law or that he should have so spoken. The question was asked in terms of Jewish law and answered in those terms. If we extend the saying of Jesus to situations which it does not cover, we should know what we are doing; the process is not illegitimate, but it requires caution. The answer of Jesus uses a rabbinical technique; the rabbis accepted an earlier verse of the Pentateuch as "weightier" than a later verse. Genesis 2:24 is "earlier" in the Pentateuch than Deuteronomy 24:1. Jesus does not annul divorce; he admits divorce as a concession to "hardness of heart." Here as elsewhere he proposes a righteousness which is more abundant than that of the Scribes and Pharisees.

Thus we find Jesus once again as usual standing with the helpless. The divorced wife in the culture of Palestinian Judaism had no place to go. In an earlier culture she might have returned to her father's house; one wonders how often this was really possible. But in Palestine of Roman times one has to ask how many father's houses could have receiveed a rejected wife. In particular one must wonder how often the abominable interpretation of Hillel was followed, and I choose the adjective deliberately. In a man's world one fears that it was the common interpretation; and one remembers that stature which Hillel had in rabbinic tradition. Jesus here spoke for the abandoned and recalled men to a sense of obligation. One may speculate—and I admit it is no more than speculation—that Jesus dismissed the interpretation of Shammai because it implied that there was no penalty laid upon the adulterous husband, and indeed there was not; the harsh laws of the Pentateuch at least made no distinction between the unfaithful husband and the unfaithful wife, but in the first century they were no longer observed. No one has ever suggested that Jesus could be invoked to support the double standard. Such a plea for those who are rejected by society is altogether in character with many savings attributed to Jesus elsewhere; he is the spokesman for the poor, the weak, the destitute, even the imprisoned. He who spoke in defense of prostitutes might have added that many prostitutes were forced into their career by the principle of the sage Hillel.

And it is just this assurance that the prohibition of divorce is quite in character that makes us wonder whether the retention of the prohibition into different ages and cultures might be unfaithful to the teachings of Jesus. Career women or women of independent wealth were known in the Hellenistic-Roman world of the New Testament, and even Jewish women of independence appeared; the New Testament mentions Herodias, Drusilla and Bernice, who are mentioned in other ancient sources and who were not oppressed or neglected. Jesus did not speak to them or on their behalf. They were hardly typical of the vast numbers of Jewish wives whose survival depended on the whim—that is not too strong a word —of their husbands. But every priest who has ever engaged in the pastoral ministry knows that the enforcement of the church prohibition of divorce in modern times is often cruel to the innocent, given that in a divorce there can be at least one party who is comparatively innocent. Nor are we speaking merely of innocent and oppressed wives; there are also innocent and oppressed husbands. We priests are aware that one must sometimes suffer for righteousness's sake; it can happen to us, rarely enough. The trouble is that priests are often made to feel like the executioner. Their proximity to the case may cloud their judgment with human sympathy; but it has never been clear that one becomes a better priest by closing one's heart to compassion. Most priests know that this feature of canon law is not the feature which is most faithfully administered. They know that when they become inhuman they step out of their priestly role. Almost no priest of my acquaintance would sit on the bench of the Inquisition; a few would. Should Jesus not have said all this? He did; but when one saying is snatched out of its context and given an importance it does not have, we make it impossible for ourselves to hear his voice.

In the belief that my fellow priests are correct in their Christian instincts, I wish to suggest a few reflections on the

prohibition of divorce—that is to say, on the indissolubility
of marriage. And the first reflection that comes to my mind is
that nowhere in the remembered sayings of Jesus does he affirm the indissolubility of marriage until death. "Till death
do us part" is a theological gloss upon marriage founded
upon something else than the words of Jesus. I suppose it is
founded upon the same natural law which permits the in-
direct killing of the innocent. By no means do I intend to
align myself with the contemporary view of marriage as a
temporary liaison which endures by mutual agreement as
long as sexual satisfaction, or something alleged to be sexual
satisfaction, is provided. Such unions lack even romantic
love. When a man and woman pledge solemnly to share their
lives, it should be a commitment with at least an intention
of permanence; otherwise the couple would profit both
themselves and society if they simply entered concubinage,
which I understand many people nowadays prefer anyway.
Concubinage is by definition a union of self-interest, while
marriage has been traditionally a union of altruism. Perhaps
it has never really fulfilled the definition; I said in an earlier
essay that I am not defending the thesis that Christian marriage has been an outstanding success in purpose and execution. But something was preserved as long as the wife was
something other than a mistress who, according to the principle of Hillel, could be dismissed if the husband found another
woman who pleased him better (meaning sexually). It is a
doubtful contribution to the dignity of woman when she is
accorded the same freedom to treat another person as a thing.

But if one is driven from the moral obscenity of divorce on
demand, one does not wish to be driven back to what has
often been the moral obscenity of no divorce at all. One
would like some way of freeing people from a character
deterioration in adult life, which is known to happen; and
while the wise elder can often by second-guessing say, "I

told you so," the young married person scarcely out of adolescence, with the experience proper to his or her age, cannot be expected to foresee such things. Must they pay a lifelong penalty for failure to see something which no one else saw? And even if the marriage was a typical heedless blunder of youth which would not have been made if they had waited until they were a few years older, is it right to attach such a long-term penalty to such a blunder of youth? I admit that this is a touchy question; certainly the young should be taught to lie in the bed they have made. The question is whether compassion permits such severity as a rule. Making marriage more difficult is far better than making divorce as easy as selling a house or a car. One does not wish to be apodictic; one wishes that in such a complex question others would avoid it also.

One cannot think of divorce and Christian marriage without attending to the union of Christ and the church proposed as the image of marriage in Ephesians 5:22-33. The image certainly does not admit divorce; Christ is not going to abandon the church, and the church cannot abandon Christ without ceasing to exist. But is this not an ideal of Christian marriage, something towards which marriage always strives without ever attaining it? Is it not something like calling the priest another Christ? I mentioned earlier that husbands of my acquaintance do not fulfil the image of Christ; I may say also that wives do not fulfil the image of the church. The marriages are none the less Christian because of the failure of the partners to fulfil the ideal. Should this image be erected into a legal code? In fact it is not. Only in the one feature of indissolubility is the image incorporated into church law. In other respects the law of the church on marriage is sufficiently realistic.

The price the church has paid for unrealism has been great. If the church had applied to the texts on divorce the same kind of exegesis it has applied to the more numerous texts on non-violence and the acquisition of wealth, divorce would be no more common in the Catholic community than war and riches. We should probably need no more to adjust to the modern world. But the refusal of the church to admit divorce meant that she was extremely tolerant of adultery, especially among the royalty and nobility. European kings had confessors who annually compelled the king to send the mistresses out of the palace during the Easter season. The church also provided bishoprics for the bastards of noblemen until a more recent modification of canon law made illegitimacy a disqualifying impediment to ordination to the episcopacy. In this moral state of affairs it is a little bit ridiculous that Henry VIII should have been excommunicated for divorce by a Pope who kept mistresses. For those of lower estate, the cities and towns of Catholic Europe provided abundant prostitution. Churchmen never reckoned the human cost of affording this satisfaction; it was part of the price of maintaining the sanctity of marriage. Or just of providing for the comfort of the male; Rabelais tells us that the theological students of Paris were regular customers of the prostitutes of the Latin Quarter.

The church has maintained its rigid no-divorce position for two thousand years; I cannot speak from personal study of the occasional exceptions which may have occurred at times. However numerous these may have been, they have certainly not affected the uniformity of the Roman tradition. The Greek churches have long accepted adultery as the sole reason for divorce; this practice is based on a faulty exegesis of Matthew 5:32 and 19:9. The strictness of the Roman tradition stands in striking contradiction to a clear permission of divorce which Paul accords in 1 Corinthians 7:12-16. It may be worth noticing that the Roman Church has consistently refused to call this divorce; it speaks of the "Pauline priv-

ilege." The divorce is not instituted by the believing partner
or by the church; it is instituted by the unbelieving partner,
and Paul recognizes the divorce so instituted. Until the twentieth century the Roman Church recognized this situation
only in marriages of two unbaptized persons one of whom
becomes a Christian; and in practice it generally meant that
the church recognized that a divorce which preceded the baptism of one of two such partners was no impediment to a
Christian marriage contracted after baptism. Paul asserted
freedom to marry on his own authority; he was aware of the
saying of Jesus forbidding divorce, and he extends the saying
to persons living under Roman law, as most of his converts
were living. But Paul believed that he had to speak to the
marriage of Christians and unbelievers, which Jesus never addressed; indeed he never addressed the subject of Christian
marriage. How could he? Paul thought that he spoke in the
spirit of Jesus when he spoke for freedom. The Roman
church, correctly interpreting Paul's declaration, has
understood that the unbelieving spouse "departs" from the
marriage when he or she refuses to "cohabit peacefully" with
the believing partner.

One may feel less assurance about a twentieth-century
expansion of the Pauline privilege which extended it to the
spouse of a Protestant. This seems to be in rather open contradiction to the traditional teaching of the Roman Church
that sacramental marriage is contracted between two baptized
persons without regard to the heresy, schism or religious inac-
tivity of one or both of them, and with its insistence since
Augustine that the validity of baptism does not depend upon
the orthodox belief either of the spouses or of the minister of
baptism. No doubt Protestants when they become aware of
this practice regard it as another example of Roman Catholic
arrogance, as well they might; it implies that the marriages of
baptized Protestants are not as sacramental as the marriages

of baptized Catholics, and that Protestants, in spite of centuries of tradition, are not really as baptized as Catholics. Effectively it places Protestants on the same religious level as the unbaptized. It is in harmony with the belief implicit in the practice of one large archdiocese, now I hope obsolete, of conditionally baptizing every baptized Protestant who became a Catholic.

But if the Roman Church may have been a bit arrogant in extending the Pauline privilege to those who entered its communion from other Christian churches, it may for once have come close to seeing that the words of Paul are not limited to marriages which founder on religious difficulties. Even the formula of canon law, which spoke of "cohabiting peacefully," is not restricted to the refusal of the unbaptized person to allow the baptized person to practice his or her religion freely. When one considers the difference in life style which the Christian undertook in the Roman world, it appears that the difference approached the difference between the religious life and the secular life in modern times. If we are right, it is easy to understand the refusal of a Roman wife or husband to continue marriage with a partner whose life and whose views had changed so radically. But Paul did not allude to this; perhaps he did not need to, but we who have so long leaned so hard on his exact words, or claim that we do, might read them. What Paul wrote was that if the unbeliever wishes to separate, he or she may do so; the believer is not bound, because God has called us to live in peace.

Would we be as much within the spirit of Paul's words as the so-called Petrine privilege if we extend them to irreconcilable differences other than those of religion? If one were to take Paul's words strictly, they would mean that a spouse who is willing to "cohabit peacefully," to borrow a phrase from the canon law, would not be bound if the spouse who were unwilling to do so had separated. But if the reasons for declaring the freedom of the abandoned spouse were limited to religious differences, we say more than Paul did. As an exegete I can go no further than that; as an exegete I think it is my duty to go that far. How much the church wishes to regulate the marriages of its members is its business; but when churchmen say or imply that what they do is based upon a biblical text, the meaning of those texts is my business.

The church seems therefore to have good biblical warrant for permitting those who have been abandoned by their spouses to remarry; this warrant it has never used. Concern for people which equaled concern for law might have moved it to act differently. Instead of divorce—which may have become easy, but it is not cheap—the church has offered her members only the possibly expensive and certainly interminable process of annulment. As one who has not studied this question closely nor been involved in the process, any reflections I might express on it would be at best shallow, and I shall abstain in the hope that others better qualified may undertake them. I understand that, if the experience of Monsignor Kelliher of the Archdiocese of New York is any guide, they had better, like me, be men whose careers are behind them and who have reached that blessed terminal serenity in which they no longer hope or fear anything men can do to them. I would be more inclined to express some reflections on the support Monsignor Kelliher received from most of his colleagues, who know he is right and who rallied behind him with all the ferocity of cornered rabbits. But those reflections must await another day, or perhaps better be suppressed entirely.

About annulments I can only say, after forty-two years in the priesthood, that there are many problems which annulments do not even meet. This I know; not with the same assurance do I say that any reform of the canonical process of annulment will also fail to meet them. What one reads about recent developments makes one wonder whether any marriage, if put under such a searching examination for flaws, could not be declared null and void. Critics of the Roman Catholic Church have said in the past that annulments could be purchased, and that the legal grounds are sometimes indistinguishable from the grounds of divorce. About such criticisms I cannot speak. It is obviously a process which the hierarchy must see as above reproach. From my own experience, I must hope that it is more above reproach than the investigation of the orthodoxy of writings and their authors.

Perhaps we return to the basic problem of Roman Catholic teaching, law and pastoral practice about marriage. It is administered by men who are celibate. There is an understanding and compassion which is gained only from sharing an experience. The most understanding and compassionate people I have known are aware of this and of where experience fails them. People who suffer find them more comforting than those who know all about it without having been there. The Catholic teaching and practice on divorce is harsh at best; its harshness is certainly in no way mitigated by the fact that those who administer this teaching and practice often seem to be unfeeling, some because they have schooled themselves to be and others because they are unfeeling. No doubt the base of teaching and pastoral practice needs to be broadened. Until that happens—and it could be a long time—those on whom the responsibility rests ought to reflect daily on all the words of Jesus, not just some of them.

Chapter Four

SUFFERING

WHEN one attempts to present some reflections on suffering, one realizes that one approaches a theme which has elicited more good and bad art, literature, poetry and drama than any other theme; and one despairs of saying anything new. In spite of all that has been said on the subject, anyone who has had to comfort the afflicted knows that it is very easy to say the one word too much, which is disastrous. When Job's friends came to comfort him, they sat in silence with him seven days and nights; this shows genuine sympathy. Once they begin to speak, the reader knows that they should have remained silent. Suffering is best considered in the quiet reflection of undisturbed tranquility; one of the things wrong with suffering is that it upsets the mind and takes away clear thinking. Theologians think calmly, most of the time, about the problem of evil, which is the problem of suffering under another name; they can think calmly as long as they can remain uninvolved.

Tragic drama, born in Greece as so many other things in our civilization were, is not certainly the beginning of the theater in the modern world; but it was the earliest form of theater of which some of the history can be traced. Tragedy is certainly a drama of suffering, but not merely of suffering. Aristotle was the first critic to say that mere suffering (you will pardon the expresison) is merely pathetic; more is required for the tragic, but what that more is has never been clear, even though most theatergoers could recognize the difference, whether they could define it or not. Theatergoers sneer at cheap playing on the emotions as tear-jerking. Tragedy is a drama of the nobility with which the human being encounters suffering and overcomes it spiritually. To borrow a line from one of my non-favorite poems, the head of the tragic hero is bloody but unbowed. Sometimes the nobility of the tragic hero is more easily called arrogance; but tragedy is not a morality play. Tragedy recognizes that man is essentially a loser, but it is possible for a few to lose with dignity. Most human suffering is simply what Aristotle called pathetic, and the creation of the tragic hero, a great creation of the imagination, does not really touch the genuine human problem. One can make theater out of Orestes, Oedipus, Antigone, Medea, Hamlet, Lear or even Macbeth; one cannot make good theater out of the captive widows of Troy or out of a thousand suicides at Jamestown or fifty refugees from Haiti drowned off the beaches of Florida, lined with luxury hotels and apartments. The pathetic is esthetically banal; and the acceptance of the cannon of tragedy as stated by Aristotle is an affirmation that almost all human suffering is meaningless.

And here we turn cruel; perhaps we do not mean to be cruel, perhaps we do not even know that we are cruel, but effectively we are. Does the tiger mean to be cruel, or know that it is cruel when it rends the lamb? Does man fall back into the state of nature? Human suffering, when it is encountered in massive quantities, stuns the mind and dulls the feelings; we become aware that our store of compassion is smaller than we thought. We can cope with a few injured, or even a few hundred; but when they appear in thousands, we employ that form of calculation known as triage. They are no longer suffering persons, they are cases; they are statistics. One may ask whether the human being is naturally compassionate toward his own kind, or whether compassion is not an acquired trait, not surely exhibited under great stress. The book of Job alludes to the common human experience of the sufferer; we turn away, we do not look, we cross the street, we pretend it is not there in the hope that it will go away. We deny that anything so offensive to sound reason and human decency can exist.

Yet men persist, as they always have, in vain efforts to make this great irrationality tolerable. The Greek adage said that one learns by suffering. The Greek was said in a cute little rhyme which I cannot reproduce in English; "from pain comes gain" is about as bad as the original in form and sentiment. Do we learn from suffering? Very few do, and most of them become so self-righteous that they add to the pain of others less strong than themselves feel. We continue the same fatuous wisdom by affirming that suffering builds character. In most cases it breaks down character and turns apparently strong men and women into whimpering objects of self-pity. A few people become beautiful in the process; for most of us becoming strong through pain offers about as much opportunity as becoming strong through a sudden demand to run twenty miles a day. A few will respond to such a demand by growth in strength; most will become tired, ill or dead. It is a sad fact that few people are improved by suffering, and it is even sadder because there is so much of it.

The biblical view of suffering is as broad as the general human view; but there are a few elements of the biblical view which are not found elsewhere. Indeed, some biblical views are nearly in direct contradiction to other biblical views. Several books of the Bible express the conviction that suffering is the consequence of human sin. This is the burden of the myths of the first eleven chapters of Genesis, not only the myth of Eden but also of the myths of Cain and Abel, of the Deluge, and of the tower of Babel. This disparate collection of myths drawn from different sources have in common the belief that man, before he became the creature known from history and experience, lived in an original state free of trouble from which he fell or was banished because he offended the deity, either collectively (as in the myths of the

Deluge and the tower of Babel) or through some representative individual (as in the myths of Eden and Cain and Abel). Man had no experience or memory of a human condition different from that of history and experience, and thus the primeval sin was located in the world of myth, beyond experience.

From this biblical mythology developed the belief in original sin. In this traditional doctrine both human sin and human suffering are attributed to a collective ancestral guilt from which Christ has delivered us. Modern man finds this belief hard to accept, probably for two reasons; it is based on mythology and not on scientific conclusions, and it seems to offend the dignity and freedom of the individual person. Space does not permit full discussion of this problem here; the belief in original sin says of the problem of suffering that it is man's fault, and that is all there is to it. This may deserve the attention even of modern man, who has rejected the myth of original sin and replaced it with the myth of the essential goodness of man. This myth is not supported by science, history or experience; and when it was erected into a theory by Pelagius in the fifth century, the church rejected it as heresy. I support this condemnation with more enthusiasm than I usually show.

The biblical myths are both like and unlike the ancestral curses of Greek mythology. Both sets of myths reflect an awareness of a guilt which is older and deeper than personal guilt. In the famous families of Greek mythology the curse, laid upon an ancestor because of some heinous crime, works itself out through several generations until the curse is expiated or the family is extinguished. Oedipus, cursed because of the guilt of an ancestor, is doomed to kill his father and marry his mother. He does both in ignorance, in spite of frantic efforts to escape the curse. The tragedy of Oedipus is that it is just those efforts to escape which put him in the position to commit both crimes. Modern readers do not appreciate the horror which the Greeks felt for parricide and incest, even done in ignorance. This is not the curse which biblical myths see laid upon mankind; the sinners of the Bible are not tragic heroes. The two mythologies agree in a conviction that the evil men do lives after them; and so they explain—or fail to explain—the suffering of the innocent. For we are offended by suffering which appears to us to be entirely undeserved; we accept, as long as we ourselves are not the guilty, suffering which comes to those who we believe have earned it. Jesus said a few things about those who pass judgment on those who deserve suffering.

Many of the biblical writers seem to explain the suffering of the innocent by the assumption that there are no innocent. This assumption is found in the myths of the Deluge and of Sodom, in which no one is spared. The assumption may have more in its favor than appears; in a question where all reasoning and logic break down ultimately, a failure of logic is no worse here than it is elsewhere. We do not criticize theories about evil because they fail in logic—they all do; we criticize them when they are manifestly unfaithful to experience. It seems to us that the myths of the Deluge and of Sodom are clearly unjust. To the ancients the gods could not be unjust; we cannot apply our standard of justice to them, and we do not know what standards they may have. One ancient Mesopotamian wise man opined that we have it backwards; what is good to us is to the gods evil, and what is evil to us is to the gods good. To the ancient Israelites a god who punished indiscriminately would be no god; only in the biblical form of the Deluge myth, as in the myth of Sodom, is it stated that all humanity, in one case, and all the inhabitants of the city, in the other, were sinners; hence the total destruction was justified. Total depravity of humanity, while not experienced, is conceivable; the hypothesis that God is unjust simply makes it impossible to think. Therefore the ancient Israelite gulped and said that in such cases the Lord is righteous in his ways, perfect in all his works.

From this simple view one can move, as many Israelite scribes did, to what scholars call the Deuteronomic theology. The name comes from the book of Deuteronomy; the theology is found there and in the historical books which were edited by scribes who impressed this theology upon their narratives. This theology affirms that a just God apportions suffering to men in proportion to their guilt. Suffering is not only the consequence of sin, a view which is entirely tenable if it is restricted to these simple terms; it is also a punishment of sin in exact proportion to the enormity of the sins of each one. The Deuteronomic theologians recognized that this explanation of suffering is contradicted by experience, which often reveals that the innocent suffer and the guilty are spared. No matter; the Deuteronomic theologians appeal to the mysterious solidarity of the human group and even of the human race as a whole, although they did not call it by that name. Children, and even more remote descendants, were punished for the sins of their parents or of their ancestors, and thus it might appear that the guilty escape and the innocent suffer. The history of Israel and Judah from the Judges to the fall of the monarchy was written in terms of this theology; to write in this way demanded some omissions and even some distortions in order that history might show, not only what did happen, but what should have happened. The writers wished to show that the accumulation of centuries of guilt made the judgments of God upon Israel and Judah entirely just. It was not totally dissimilar to the Greek understanding of the ancestral curse; and both the myth of the curse and the Deuteronomic theology are early instances of the theory of guilt by association. Men have always believed in guilt by association, and we still believe in it. It makes it easier to bear the irrational burden of suffering.

The Deuteronomic theology is the wisdom of Job's friends, caricatured but not distorted beyond recognition. Job shows clearly that the theory breaks down against experience, and that it fails to explain the real and poignant suffering of the individual person. Job does not deny the mysterious fact of ancestral guilt; he says it is irrelevant. What does the wicked care if the punishment of his sins is visited upon his descendants long after he is dead? Nor does it comfort the afflicted to tell them that they suffer not from their own fault, but from guilt by association. Job tells his friends that to assert that all suffering is deserved, either by personal guilt or by guilty associations, is to tell lies on God's behalf.

Before we dismiss the theory of Job's friends too hastily, let us take time to reflect that they speak for all of us. The naked fact of simple human anguish with no perceptible cause is intellectually so difficult and emotionally so repulsive that our instant reaction is to say that it is not real, and perhaps we never move beyond that refusal to accept reality. We say that "they" do not really feel pain. Or, if we are forced to accept the fact, we manufacture for "them" resources of tolerance which we do not have; "they" have never had much, or "they" never expected much, or "they" do not know what they are missing, or "they" are insensitive. All of these are frantic efforts to distance ourselves from the sufferer. Or when we cannot evade suffering by flight, we take refuge in the theology of Job's friends and affirm, without much reference to reality, that after all "they" deserve it. "They" are reaping their wild oats, their own or their parents. The disciples once asked Jesus who had sinned, this man or his parents, that he should be born blind. They committed an intolerable logical fallacy, but no worse than we usually commit when we are confronted with the revolting fact of suffering. "They" are heedless or improvident, "they" are not industrious, "they" are not ambitious, "they" are not satisfied with limited ambitions, "they" are not trustworthy—for these and for any other reasons we can find, they are in trouble. The only reason, really, is that they are not like us.

I have dwelt on the pronoun "they" because all these rationalizations of suffering are applicable only to the suffering of others. When we suffer, we are innocent victims, and we see at once with marvelous clarity the fallacy of the Deuteronomic theology. It might be a sudden comfort—to others, if not to ourselves—if we said when we suffer that it could not happen to a more deserving person; and we might be less of a nuisance to those whom duty or affection compels to assist us. Whether we could ever become so well adjusted that we could make their ministry an agreeable task I cannot be sure; I observed earlier that most of us do not know what a pain in the neck we become when we suffer. There are, of course, exceptions; we recognize and honor them. In general nothing extinguishes compassion as quickly as self-pity. Even the book of Job, which is great literature by any standards, sometimes offends readers because of what they think is a sustained querulous tone. The same disagreeable note is struck in many of what are called the Psalms of personal lament. No doubt the Psalms and Job do express the universal cry of mankind in pain, but we do not want to be reminded that others are in pain. It occurs to me that suffering degrades not only those who suffer but also those who witness suffering; in either case our humanity is diminished.

The Old Testament theology of suffering rises to its climax in the book of Job. Job, after exploring in the dialogue with his friends almost every angle from which suffering can be contemplated, reaches no insight which makes suffering rationally acceptable and emotionally tolerable. Job concludes only with a belief that one must accept God as greater than suffering, that one must trust God totally to make sense out of nonsense, and that one must permit God to do it his own way. To believe that even God cannot make sense out of suffering is to grant in despair that human life is a tale told by an idiot, full of sound and fury, signifying nothing. Much is made nowadays of the denial that there are any absolutes. Let us consider what the denial involves. Certainly the constant and losing struggle to alleviate human suffering is one of the alleged absolutes which we can easily do without.

So we come to the theology of the cross, which in Christian teaching has almost always been the theology of the cross and the crown. Indeed a theology of the cross without the crown would be intolerable. Suffering becomes tolerable if there is an assurance that it is rewarding, and I mean rewarding to the sufferer, not to someone else. Job was neither the first nor the last to ask what posterity meant to him. The theology of the cross and crown is a simple faith and hope, and Jesus presents himself as our example and assurance. This simple faith and hope have sustained many; and I wonder whether my duty as theologian compels me to complicate something which has proved itself both simple and successful. Perhaps we theologians think too much; I have often been told that I need less thought and more prayer. The much abused "simple faithful" cope with life without the assistance of theological thinking.

But do they cope with life? Not always and everywhere; the theology of the cross and the crown, simple as it is, needs a better explanation than it often gets. We expositors ought to remember that the theology of the cross may show people how to live; it does not solve problems or answer questions. Whether it be the message or the messenger, the theology of the cross sometimes repels those who suffer. I have said above that it does not set one up for clear thinking. Certainly the moments of anguish are not the time to be told that suffering is beautiful, that it is constructive, that it builds up and matures Christian character, that it confers insight into the reality of God. Such tactless remarks exacerbate the native hostility which the sufferer feels toward anyone who is not in pain. The sufferer can respond to compassion, but an essential component is "passion." To feel the pain of others is really a rare gift, but it can be acquired. Without this gift the gospel of the cross is sounding brass and tinkling cymbals.

To ask how much control Jesus had over his state of life would lead to a discussion of Christology which, I think, most Catholic theologians would find embarrassing. Let us say that he was a member of the underprivileged class, which formed perhaps 95% of the population of the Roman Empire. As a member of this class, what has been esteemed as the good life was totally out his reach. It may be significant that the elite who enjoyed the good life did so only at the cost of a vast amount of suffering endured by others; that may still be true, even if the elite is larger, but that is another question. If we know anything about the teaching of Jesus— I bow in deference to my learned colleagues—he taught nothing about how the good life should be made more widely available to the poor, the meek, the lowly, the victims of injustice, and the others who are called fortunate in the beatitudes. The usual means by which men escape suffering he not only did not recommend, he positively rejected. He seems to have said that the good life is not what most people think it is, that it can be achieved even by the underprivileged and the disadvantaged, and that it is available now. Lazarus will not achieve the good life by becoming as rich as Dives; he can achieve it if he remains Lazarus.

Is this not close to saying what has often been said of Christianity, that it is a gospel which teaches the poor to be content with their poverty? Again, if we know anything at all about the words of Jesus, we know that he was not indifferent to human pain. Fear of compromising his divinity has often kept Christians from seeing how deeply human pain entered into his soul. Jesus never said that suffering is not real, or that it does not hurt much, or that it passes quickly, or that it is good for you. He seems to have recommended something too simple, which does not touch the theoretical problem of suffering. His response to suffering was: stop hurting each other. That much anyone can do; if you cannot do that much, do not form a study group. If one believes anything about Jesus, one knows that he was deeply and personally involved with people, more deeply than anyone who ever lived; it is blasphemy to suggest that he was cold or unfeeling or could ever have thought that people, like eggs, had to be broken for a good cause.

Jesus said nothing about suffering; he simply embraced it as his human portion. His disciples saw in this act a saving value compared to which other saviors who save men by war, politics, liberation, healing, or any of the conventional modes of heroism are nothing. Jesus did not embrace the Deuteronomic theology; he did seem to say that man cannot overcome suffering. He must first overcome himself, and even that he cannot do unless he trusts God completely. The good life is achieved by denying that one's self is worth saving. Paul said that the life of the Christian is to suffer and die with Christ. Most of us have thought that the Christian life is to enjoy what the redeeming death has accomplished but never, never to share in it. The redeeming death cannot mean that we must modify our way of life if it is maintained at the cost of the suffering of others.

No, Jesus did not really solve the problem of evil; it remains as much of a riddle as ever. Possibly he has taught, as no one else ever did, where the problem lies. I cannot be sure that evil would vanish from the world if the Gospel were believed and lived; I know that it has never been preached, let alone believed and lived, and that one one can say it has been tried and failed (acknowledgements to Chesterton). I do know that Jesus has shown what one individual, no matter how small and insignificant he or she may be, can do to overcome evil where he or she meets it. I know that he has shown that complete human fulfillment is altogether independent of all the things which we associate with the good life. Does Mother Teresa live the good life?

Chapter Five

SEXUAL MORALITY
Part I

WHEN this book was planned, it was suggested that several essays on sexual morality be included. I accede to this suggestion, not without hesitation. I am not sure that the prospective readers are eager for more statements on sexual morality, or that they ought to be; but I would have to be totally detached from the contemporary scene not to know that there is a great deal of interest in this topic, or that there is thought to be. I feel no inner necessity to communicate any message on the most discussed of all moral topics—and the most fruitlessly discussed, if one judges from assured and generally accepted conclusions. I have for many years had a sneaking suspicion—in my later years perhaps not so sneaking—that the public is fed up with clergymen who seem to feel compelled to speak and write on this topic. If they are Catholic priests, they cannot know anything about it except by hearsay, as long as they are what they pretend to be; and hearsay does not qualify one as an expert. The student of the Bible, if he stays with his subject to any depth, cannot miss the fact that the remembered words of Jesus contain almost nothing on questions of sexual morality. If he is a student of Roman Catholic theology, he cannot miss the fact that sexual morality has a larger place in moral and pastoral instruction than anything else. One would think that this might create a problem; that students of theology might wonder whether they should not place the moral and pastoral emphasis where Jesus laid it. It is not hard to find. But in my generation we were so brainwashed on the topic of magisterium that we easily brushed aside such suspicions. One of the effects of a good brainwashing is: to avoid asking the wrong questions, don't ask any questions.

One finds the same reticence in the other books of the New Testament; and the reticence becomes more surprising as one learns about the world in which the Gospels and the New Testament were written. I came to the study of the Bible after an amount of reading in Latin and Greek authors which would have given me a good start on a doctor's degree. I was nowhere near what someone called the grammarian Friedrich Blass, an Athenian ghost, but I was more at home in that world than most of my contemporaries; and I was at home enough to wonder why the New Testament adverted so little to the almost total absence of any restraint of the sexual impulses which prevailed in the Hellenistic-Roman world. I still think—it is debatable—that the unrestrained licentiousness of the Roman world was even greater than that of the modern western world. The reason for thinking so is that the modern world is at least post-Christian; it has known, not very effectively, the restraints of Christian morality, and still pays some grudging tribute to people who have risen above the moral gutter. But the Roman world was pre-Christian; it had never known any restraint except the faded ethics of the Roman Republic and the Stoic ethics of an aristocratic elite. In the cities, towns and villages of the Mediterranean world of the first century, the prostitute rendered a social service as useful as the service of the barber, and a visit to one was as morally significant as a visit to the other. The wealthy sought and achieved more spectacular forms of diversion, which we read about in the satirists; some of them were too strong even for Roman tastes. But the worst a Roman could say about them was that they were in bad taste. Paul had the material to write like Juvenal; he did not. The reticence of the New Testament about sexual morality does not arise from the absence of the problem. One has to appeal to the innocence and ignorance of the writers, which no one has done, as far as I know; so perhaps we should conclude that they talked about things they thought were more important—or at least more urgent.

Jesus, of course, did not live in the heart of the Hellenistic-Roman world; he lived in the world of Palestinian Judaism. The character which I have attempted to sketch of the morality of the larger world is not valid for Palestinian Judaism. It was a remote and backward corner of the Roman world, and contemporary writers tell us, whether they intend to or not, that Judaism was regarded by the Gentiles as a quaint and eccentric if harmless religion. Gentiles noticed other things about Jews besides their abstinence from pork and the practice of circumcision. They also noticed the strict moral regime which governed Jewish marriage and sexual relations. This obvious contrast with the Gentile world means of itself no more than the strictness of Victorian morality in contrast with the looseness of eighteenth-century England. Hypocrisy is the tribute which vice pays to virtue, a tribute which contemporary vice is unwilling to pay. Neither did the Hellenistic-Roman world pay this tribute. Jews of the time expressed a savage contempt for the laxness of Gentile morals, a contempt which occasionally finds expression in the New Testament; it is something like the unconscious ethnic prejudice so often found in the speech and writing of those who belong to no minority group. We can conclude that Jesus did not find as much occasion to mention sexual morality as he would have found if he had lived in Rome, Alexandria or Antioch—or Corinth, a small city, celebrated for its vice. I point out that the New Testament writers who did live in those places did not mention it much more.

Catholic moral and pastoral teaching has long been governed by a principle which I feel the need to discuss; the reasons for this personal need will shortly become clear. I do not know where it would be placed in a more orderly treat-

ment; but I am not sure that this treatment pretends to much
of any kind of order. Hence it will clear my mind if no one
else's mind if I take it up here. The principle of which I speak
was enunciated in Latin when I studied theology; I render it,
perhaps somewhat roughly, thus: in sexual activity, whether
alone or with others, even if limited to thought or inneffective
desires, as long as there is activity of the sexual organs, there
is no slightly or venially sinful matter. This means that any
physical sexual activity, even solitary or incipient, is serious
matter, gravely or mortally sinful, excused from serious malice only by lack of reflection or of full consent of the will.
Catholics were taught, even before the awakening of sexual
consciousness, that any thought, word or action, even the
slightest physical reaction, was a mortal sin unless it were in-
stantly suppressed. No one knows how many Catholics were
tortured by that mental disease called "scruples" as a result
of this teaching. They felt they were hopelessly damned to
hell unless they could get rid of their bodies. Most priests had
to deal with these afflicted persons at some time; they could
tell them anything except the one thing that would relieve
them, that not all physical reactions deserved to be evaluated
as serious sins. Most priests told such penitents to stop worry-
ing about it; it was regarded as good pastoral advice to tell
them not to confess such things. This good advice rarely
worked. Normal people thought or were told that most of
their sexual experiences were indeliberate or half-hearted.
In one way or another priests and people lived as if the
theological consent about the seriousness of sexual material
did not exist. If they did not so live, they fell into scruples.
Matters were not helped by proposing an entirely fictitious
Virgin Mary as spared from the curse of concupiscence, a
privilege which was granted to a few other saints—including
Thomas Aquinas, the patron of theologians. Really good
people like those did not have to fight temptation, they did

not even feel it. Stories of other heroic saints, not too well authenticated, related how by divine inspiration they lived in happy continence for years of marriage. No wonder most of the laity were left feeling like fugitives from a sty for not attaining such heights of grandeur.

Once one realizes what a simplistic denial of the realities of human psychophysiology is involved in this teaching, one begins to wonder on what it is based. A former colleague of mine, John R. Connery, made the history of this question the topic of his doctoral dissertation; I have never seen the published results of this work, and if I have missed it I apologize. But there is no authority for this teaching in the Bible or in authentic Catholic teaching. It enjoys the status of a commonly accepted theological opinion, and one is censured for rashness for departing from such opinion. At my age rashness is no longer the risk which one once thought it was. One needs more than a long-established and uncritically accepted theological opinion to do what one fears is to bind intolerable burdens on people without lifting a finger to raise them. Jesus did indeed say, or is credited with saying, that one who looks lustfully upon a woman has already committed adultery with her in his heart. He made a similar remark about one who is angry with his brother or uses abusive language, but the theologians have not agreed that any sentiment of anger, even slight, is material of grave sin. Murder in the heart is quite bad, and Jesus said it is, but it is not the same thing as murder in deed. Theologians have said that adultery in the heart is the same thing as adultery in deed. If it is rash to say that this no longer goes, then I have to be rash. I trust I make it clear that I am not supporting any insinuation that evil desires, even those which are ineffective, are morally meaningless. Jesus also said that all the evil in the human person comes from the heart.

With the resources available at this writing I am unable to

trace with any thoroughness the origin and development of this theological opinion. I do know that one large religious community of men imposed this opinion upon its members by its Institute; at least this was true fifteen years ago. I have not heard of any change in this respect since. There may be other communities which by rule or custom impose the same opinion; about them I do not know. The community of which I have some knowledge has for a few hundred years produced a series of celebrated teachers and writers of moral theology, and so its influence has been far greater than its numbers; its former students long included bishops, cardinals, popes, and professors of theology. This alone may not explain the tenacity with which the opinion was held; it certainly goes a long way.

Yet the opinion reeks of the ancient heresy of Manichaeism. This heresy was a form of the bewildering variety of heretical eccentricities lumped as Gnosticism. Several forms of this heresy proclaimed that the flesh and all its works were evil; that the fall of man consisted in his incarnation; that his salvation was accomplished not by freedom from sin but by becoming a pure spirit. The heresy spawned several legends of virgin martyrs who gladly suffered death when at divine inspiration they renounced their husbands on their wedding night. If these legends had any credibility, the persecution of Christians by Romans would be easy to explain. In the seventeenth and eighteenth centuries the heresy was revived with new vigor as Jansenism, which was strong in France, Italy and Ireland. Oddly enough, the religious community mentioned above was one of the stoutest adversaries of Jansenism, which counted a large number of bishops among its supporters. One wonders whether the Jansenists, like some other famous contenders, did not win the war in spite of losing all the battles.

There is, however, much to be said for the long tradition of

Catholic moral theology, in spite of its unsavory roots and its sad consequences for the individual conscience. We must remember the casual morality of sex which we reviewed in the Hellenistic-Roman civilization; and we must remember also that western Christian culture has at no period of its history since Constantine been a model of sexual moderation and restraint. In particular the period of the Renaissance of the fifteenth century was a time of increased relaxation under the influence of the revival of classical literature after the relatively rigorous morality of the Middle Ages. The stance which Catholic moral theology adopted may have been exaggerated and wrong, but it is easy to understand as an excessive reaction; it was not unlike the moral majority of the contemporary scene, about which I shall have more to say later. The moral and pastoral theologians were reacting against a moral practice which accepted concubinage as normal among the clergy at all levels of rank. A recent historian of venereal disease has calculated that three popes within twenty-five years around the turn of the sixteenth century can be proved to have exhibited the symptoms of syphilis. One understands the difficulty which some felt in presenting the Catholic Church as a moral leader in anything. That should not condemn Catholics of following centuries to live with their overzealous mistakes.

The contemporary church at least does not have the embarrassment of such moral degradation in its official leadership. I have not read *The Cardinal Sins,* by Andrew Greeley, nor do I intend to. Some reviewers have thought it necessary to warn the readers that Greeley does not intend to describe the contemporary clergy. He certainly did not describe the clergy I know, as far as I can gather from the reviews; but how many of the clergy does anyone know? Enough to be sure that we do not live in the Renaissance, and that the church can take a strong moral position without embarrassment. But it cannot take a strong position which is based upon reality. The strong position which can be taken and seriously maintained has simply not been formulated as of yet; by seriously I mean a line of conduct which can be recommended as practical.

One returns again to the reticence of the New Testament on this topic; and one is impressed by the fact that when the church attempted to go beyond this reticence, it said too much. There are often moral areas on which we find the New Testament lacking; it seems unaware of the problems we have and it does not answer our questions. Where the New Testament was found lacking, answers were sought in the ethics of the natural law; perhaps this was necessary although one sees arising a class of Christian scribes, not well-versed, like Ezra, in the law of Moses, but in the law of nature. If Jesus had wanted moral direction by experts it was already in existence. Its representatives, according to the Gospels, thought Jesus was hostile to them. Paul certainly did not regard himself as a founding member of a new class of moral experts. Perhaps I have been wrong in writing for some years that Jesus, at least as understood in the Gospels and by Paul, seemed to wish to create individual persons who would be able to make their own moral judgments. I find nothing in the Gospels of that docile attitude which says, "Do not compel us to decide what is right; you tell us what to do."

The ethics of the law of nature have really been the ethics of the culture of western Europe, now transplanted to other continents as well. The human nature on which these ethics were based was really a very limited sample of humanity; how limited it was Europeans never knew until the sixteenth century, and then it took another three hundred years to realize that those whom they had called savages, natives or barbarians and dismissed as subhuman were fully as human as themselves. What we have learned is that sexual activity is governed by social convention everywhere; theologians have tried to impose the social conventions of western Europe upon humanity as the ethics of the natural law, with a lack of success which is not surprising. It is neither smart nor sophisticated to dismiss conventional morality as based on no thought and without value. To say that it should be replaced by the free choice of consenting adults is to invite moral chaos, and it is probably safe to say that society will never accept that. Sexual behavior is governed by convention in all human societies, not only in western European; and no one has yet discovered a society which permits consenting adults to exercise their free choice without restraint. One may say that some conventional morality appears to be natural, if universality is the test; but there are very few particular restraints of convention which are universal.

If it is conventional morality and not the immutable laws of nature which we are talking about, must we not face the possibility that there will be evolution in this area of morality as there is evolution in other areas? In earlier essays I have discussed the changes which the changing status of women introduces into the mores of divorce. Thus I seem to have answered my own question. But one knows that a social consensus is slow to emerge and, once emerged, is even slower to change. I respond to cries about a "new morality" about the way a bull responds to a red flag; I suppose that is what my friends mean when they say I am hopelessly conservative. A new morality does not emerge like this year's fashions. That morality develops at all, but does so very slowly, ultimately must be attributed to the fact, noted by W. S. Gilbert, that every little boy and girl born into this world alive is born a little Liberal or a little Conservative. What emerges from the present discussion is that, whether we are little Liberals or little Conservatives, it is social conventions and not the eternal law revealed by God through Jesus Christ which is under discussion. And in modern times a few words said in behalf of conventional morality may not be said amiss.

It was either Aldous Huxley or Evelyn Waugh who wrote about fifty years ago that American college boys and girls copulated with the easy frequency of dogs. These boys and girls were the people of my own age group, the generation of the flapper and the lounge lizard, now remembered only by a few of us antiques. Those boys and girls are the grandparents of the present generation of students. I will not pass on modern students the same judgment passed upon their grandparents; I do not know enough about them. Being literate, I am aware that others have done so. If the contemporary judgment is correct, one must admit that the students moved into a tradition of promiscuity of the campus which goes back to the 1920s. It was Dorothy Parker who said, I think about 1930, that if all the girls at Yale prom were laid end to end, she would not be surprised. And since the upper or ruling class generally sets the moral tone in any society, are we witnessing the emergence of a new set of social conventions? And is not the pace slow enough to mute even the most cautious conservative? The answer to this question will take up most of the remaining essays which I have set aside for this topic.

Ultimately I shall not base my remarks upon social conventions, except to the degree where one must unconsciously do so; these are part of learning to be a human being and a member of a particular society. One cannot put them off any more than one can put off one's language; it is possible, but difficult. I said above that Jesus seemed to have in mind a person able to make his own moral decisions, free from undue pressures either from within, from personal desires and interests, or from without, from fear or human respect or the desire to please. Such persons in the New Testament are not expected to be solitary agents lost in a hostile society. They are members of a community which, however small, furnishes light on obscure moral decisions and moral support against the loneliness of those whose convictions are rejected by the majority. If there is a Christian morality of sex, it is a morality of convention; the convention here expresses the moral consensus of the Christian community. It seems to me, if I may say so with due reverence (perhaps I cannot), that the official leadership of the Christian community has not furnished the necessary consensus. It has failed to find a positive way of teaching sexual morality; it has followed the traditional (and I mean Jansenistic) attitude of do not speak, do not touch, it is a dirty thing and as good Catholics you ought to rise above it. I suppose Catholics have been too timid to say they are not that good, and certainly too timid to tell their leaders they are not that good either.

I certainly have no delusions that I will here or elsewhere fill what is so obviously missing in traditional Catholic moral and pastoral teaching. At the risk of being tediously repetitious, it is high time that literate married people become a part of the moral teaching of the church concerning sexual morality. Should this happen before I die, I will not find it necessary to read what they produce and I will be spared the composition of such pieces as this.

Chapter Six

SEXUAL MORALITY
Part II

IN the last chapter I adverted to the fact that the Catholic Church has known in the past sex scandals in the life of the clergy. I said that I believe the freedom of the church from such scandals in the present makes it possible for the church to take a firm stand against the totally relaxed sexual mores of western culture. It does not make it easy; nothing makes it easy to take such a stand. I also adverted to the unfortunate fact that the church has made its own task more difficult by taking some unjustified rigid positions. Some of these I shall attend to in the course of this and the following chapter. First I wish to discuss briefly the problem of clerical celibacy. His Holiness John Paul II has made it clear that he will entertain no change in this practice nor even any discussion of change; and what I say here will not establish my filial loyalty to the Holy Father. I regret that my idea of responsibility to the church is not synonymous with a narrow conception of personal loyalty to the Holy Father. Such a loyalty relieves one of a lot of thought, and makes things much easier. But somehow I believe the church is bigger than he is, and I am aware of the risks involved in so believing.

My observation, limited as it is, has been that Catholic priests are substantially faithful to their obligation of celibacy. In the modern western world this is so remarkable an idea that most people simply do not believe that priests are what they claim to be. It is assumed *a priori* that they cannot be. A prominent Catholic, now deceased, was quoted as saying that he got headaches in the afternoon if he did not have sexual intercourse after lunch, with his wife or another. In a world where such a Gargantuan appetite is accepted as normal and not pathological, the celibate priest is as incredible as a square circle. Yet in the village community of the parish the priest lives in a goldfish bowl. And when it must perforce be recognized that there are celibate priests, the conclusion drawn by the sophisticated is that they are abnormal, especially when they seem to get through the afternoon without headaches. The profession of clerical celibacy, even imperfectly observed, is a silent but clear protest to the western world that its abandonment of sexual restraint does not arise from any genuine psychological or biological need. It says that men and women have sex without restraint for the same reason for which they show no restraint in eating, drinking liquor, taking drugs or doing violence to each other.

Where, then, do I think I may be disloyal to the Holy Father? I differ precisely because he seems to think that priests should be obliged to make this renunciation. I do not dispute that the discipline of clerical celibacy has been enforced in the Latin Church for nearly a thousand years. The only choice has been to become or not to become a priest; if one elected the priesthood, one elected celibacy. Nor do I dispute whether the practice had or had not solid foundations in the needs of the church at the time. I do insist, and no recent studies have shown anything else, that clerical celibacy is a purely ecclesiastical—that is, human—institution, that it can be changed by the same authorities which instituted it for what are judged to be good reasons. I think that those good reasons exist and should be presented; and I do not admit ignorance either of the realities of celibacy nor of its alleged theological foundation. That, I take it, makes me disloyal.

It has long been clear to me that compulsion is foreign to the Gospel. I do not say that this is so clear that I can show it beyond dispute to those who do not see it. Nor do I deny that some element of compulsion may be necessary in any social structure; I say only that where we think we find it necessary, we are depending on something basically unchristian. The Gospels tell us that Jesus invited disciples to a close association with him. This was a free association. The only condition which we find imposed is hardly a condition; it is a total renunciation of self, of family, of possessions, of worldly security. Obviously the church has never institutionalized this condition for its clergy; why does it pick on celibacy, not practiced almost certainly by Peter and by some others of the Twelve? The renunciation of discipleship can hardly be achieved by a single stroke; it is fulfilled by fidelity to a life-long commitment, of whose demands one grows daily more deeply aware. If the saying of Matthew 19:10-12 about making oneself a eunuch for the kingdom of heaven had any reference to clerical celibacy—which it does not—it would state an option for those who choose it. I shall return to this saying shortly.

Since we are now turning to New Testament texts, let us remember that the distinction of clergy and laity was unknown to the writers of the New Testament. Any declaration which celibacy makes to an oversexed world is shared by all the disciples according to their state, married or single, clerical or lay. The text about those who make themselves eunuchs for the kingdom of heaven says that any disciple in any state of life may encounter a crisis in which the kingdom of heaven may be secured only by total renunciation of sex. I observed in an earlier essay that the New Testament does not attend much to our topic, although it is hard to see why it should have been less urgent then than we think it is now. But if we attach as much value to Jesus' words as preserved in the Gospels as we say we do, we ought to give those few texts which are relevant close attention.

It so happens that the sayings attributed to Jesus are found in the Gospel of Matthew without parallel in Mark and Luke.

In modern criticism this does not mean that they are not sayings of Jesus; it does mean that one has greater difficulties in showing it to one who denies it. I mentioned in an earlier essay the saying that one who looks at a woman lustfully commits adultery in the heart (Matthew 5:27-28). I remarked that it is a misunderstanding of this saying to make the sin of desire as malicious as the sin of deed. Yet it is clear the righteousness above the righteousness of the Law is not achieved simply by avoiding the deed. That the saying deals with adultery and not other carnal sins recognized in Jewish society as such is true; to make anything out of it is nitpicking —straining out a gnat, to borrow a phrase. The point of the saying is clearly that one surely avoids adultery if one does not even think about it. Jesus says elsewhere (Mark 7:14-15; Matthew 15:17-19) that all evil begins in the heart. This seems to restate a fairly sound, even banal, psychological principle that what is much in anyone's thoughts, desires and speech is generally in one's actions.

It can probably be said safely that we do not live in a clean world. I think I am as aware as anyone else of what the Moral Majority might do. The story of my life, which I am not going to tell, includes the recital of a number of losses, financial and in reputation, incurred by refusals to submit to people who tried to tell me how to think and how to speak and write. I am still unrepentant. I know the Moral Majority is a threat. I see them arrayed against another equally menacing threat. One can only say that in this combat good men and women will suffer no matter who wins. In spite of pressures, I am going to remain neutral. And since no one will dispute that the Moral Majority is a threat, let me explain why I fear the opposing threat; why I feel like the man mentioned by the prophet Amos who escaped from a lion only to meet a bear. The media of communication seem to have fallen into the hands of men and women who have the ethics of whoremongers. They bleat that their civil liberties are threatened if they are forbidden to sell dirty pictures to children. If all they wanted was the protection of their constitutional right to scribble obscene words on the walls of public buildings, I suppose I should have to bear it. A priest in New York operates on a shoestring a mission for the reclaiming of adolescent girl runaways who are prostituted by the thousands in New York alone every year. No one but Father Bruce Ritter and the few who support him seem to think that this is more of a threat than campaigns to keep an obscene movie off TV. May I timidly suggest that one thing that comes to mind from Matthew 5:27-28 is that the sex industry is all of one piece? But the producers and directors and performers of what is called kiddie porn whine that it is not we who are pimping. No, we are for art and we demand the sacred freedom of the artist. Maybe so, but watching TV never gives me the illusion that I am strolling in the Uffizi. The porn in the Uffizi is at least executed with good technique. One can pass it and go on. If I try to tell someone as publicly as in these essays that most TV is not worth watching, I may be in trouble with the ACLU.

The text of Matthew 5:27-30 goes on to suggest rather violent means of protecting oneself against inner corruption; the violence is not directed toward others. The church has never taken this text as literally as it has taken the text on divorce. The speech of Jesus is popular, at times earthy, and it should be so understood. In most texts this has rarely created a problem for the reader or the interpreter. The text of Matthew 19:12 may allude to the self-castrated devotees of the goddess Cybele; the third century theologian Origen erred grievously when he took the text literally. If I say, "I would not do that for a million dollars," it expresses a firm unwillingness which should be taken seriously; it is not a basis for haggling about price. The saying of Matthew 5:29-30 certainly means that there should be no dirt which we cherish above the possession of a clean mind. The saying of Matthew 19:12 certainly means that the Christian vocation may demand a total renunciation of sex (as the *New American Bible,* avoiding both earthy language and the exegetical trap into which Origen fell, has rendered it). One does not cherish a clean mind by professing such rot as "To the pure all things are pure."

But what is a clean mind? The easy answer is to say that a prudish mind is a clean mind. At my age, at least, one has learned that this is not true. One must live with the reality of sex, and if one is to live with it retaining some shreds of human decency one must live with it somewhat easily. The prude lives with it in constant discomfort which he or she communicates to everyone within earshot. The prude is unhappy with his or her sex—a basic Gnostic response—and resents it when others are not equally unhappy with theirs. Their mission they conceive to be to spread discomfort and fear. Yet how does one formulate the difference between a healthy joy in one's body and the sleazy suggestiveness of a Jordache commercial? When one hears people of different ages, sexes, religious beliefs and degrees of educational advance say with one voice, "That's vile," how much theorizing does one need? To the pure, *Fanny Hill* is not pure. To give Mr. John Cleland what little honor is due him, he never said it was.

We come back, it seems, to social convention as the ultimate guide. Social conventions vary too widely from time to time and place to place to furnish a basis for hard and fast rules. In an earlier essay I pointed out that one treats them as meaningless or valueless at one's peril. The conventions deserve respect and no more. Unconventional behavior has no more in its favor antecedently than conventional behavior. If one wishes to attract attention or express one's individuality, unconventional behavior is the cheapest and the least

demanding way of doing it; one suggests to the unconventional that they would do better to write a book, paint a picture or compose a symphony, all of which, even moderately
well done, will more surely and permanently attract attention
and express individuality. That the conventions ever inhibited
authentic genius from performing needs to be shown me. In
forming a clean mind the conventions furnish a guide neither
safe nor sure, and subject to modification, but a better guide
than the adolescent desire to show off. I am long impatient
with the display of unconventional behavior as a substitute
for non-existent talent.

It seems or should seem beyond dispute that the young
must be taught the conventions. It does not seem that they
are self-taught or communicated by the peer group of the
young. I say it should be beyond dispute; apparently it is not.
To many of my contemporaries the greatest threat to the
young is that they will be inhibited. I read a metropolitan
newspaper nearly every day, and I read about young people
who, to an old curmudgeon, seem to need inhibition as much
as they need anything else. I suppose they more obviously
need love. That is certainly true; they would not have grown
up ignorant of how to live if they had ever experienced it. But
is there not a fallacy in believing that love never imposes inhibitions? We should have learned that yielding to each and
every desire of another is not love; and perhaps this is what
has been presented to so many of these young people as love.
No wonder they do not know what it means. There is an ancient and widespread belief, older than the Bible and ranging
through all human cultures, that the way to teach children to
live with sex is not to allow them free use of it as if it were a
toy. I fail to see that the invention of the computer or of jet-
propelled aircraft has cast doubt on this belief.

A New Testament text which I find bears upon my topic is
found in Paul's First Epistle to the Corinthians 6:12-20. The

reader should know that Corinth enjoyed a reputation for lewdness which stood out even in the Roman-Hellenistic world, though some scholars have questioned whether the Corinth of Paul's time still enjoyed that reputation. But it was a Roman, not a Greek proverb which said that Corinth is not a place for everyone to visit. Corinth was a busy seaport, and the reputation of ports has not changed much since the Phoenicians went down to the sea in ships. Paul urges his Christians to shun what seems to have been the socially acceptable practice from the motive that their bodies are temples of the Holy Spirit, and that their bodies are members of the body of Christ; to fornicate is to make the members of the body of Christ one body with a prostitute. The language is strong enough. One wonders whether Paul is alluding to the famous temple of Aphrodite which once stood in Corinth; it had a staff of a thousand prostitutes. In any case, he could hardly have put the issue more clearly; the Christian believes that his body is the temple of the Holy Spirit, the Pagan believes his body is the temple of Aphrodite. Which God do you worship? As Elijah said to the Israelites, make up your minds.

I write this presumably for Christian readers who profess that they share Paul's belief that their bodies are members of Christ and temples of the Holy Spirit. I simply do not know how many will find Paul's application of this belief to sexual conduct meaningful. I fear that if I expand beyond Paul's words, which, as I said, are strong enough, I would become unpardonably crude. But Paul goes through six verses to make it clear to his readers that illicit sex is a profanation of what they believe to be most sacred. I think he may have been clear enough for them. Your sophisticated modern will ask with a sneer, "What is illicit sex?" I suppose to such I have nothing to say. Paul did, but they would find his language abusive and lacking understanding. If sex is as meaningful morally as a game of tennis (echoing a once famous line) or the theater or dinner, then it is as meaningful and as impersonal as the coupling of dogs and cats.

What Paul said as strongly as he knew how was that the casual sex-for-pay of the brothel was degrading to the person. Perhaps we must find a new way of saying this in an age when the freedom of the individual person to do his or her own thing has become the most basic and the most sacred of rights. John Garvey in *Commonweal* recently wrote about a right-to-choice advertisement that the advertisement makes the choice itself and only the choice important; you have a choice, therefore you have a God-given right to exercise it. It makes no difference what the choice is. Mr. Garvey adds that he sees no reason why one should not say that you have a choice to practice child-abuse, therefore you have a God-given right to exercise it. Of course, he goes on, the defenders of the right to choose will say that there are other parties involved in child-abuse, and this limits your choice. Applying Mr. Garvey's treatment to sexual freedom, we may observe that except where solitary vice is concerned, which for the moment I omit from discussion, for sex it always takes two to tango. If one wishes to degrade his own person, there is no question that it is his person; I may demand that he not be a public nuisance. But the defenders of sexual freedom make much of the principle that they defend the freedom of two consenting adults to do as they please. I will let them deal with the problem that neither in sexuality nor in anything else does social convention allow two consenting adults to do whatever they please. Society assumes, sometimes overgenerously, that one or two of any number of consenting adults can be trusted to impose the restraints of reason and common sense upon their liberties.

Everyone is against rape, at least no one admits to being for it; but women tell us that men on the bench, on the police force and on juries are strangely sympathetic to other men. They are inclined to treat rape as a seduction by the female. Since my youth I have been startled by the number of men who asume that they would do any woman a favor by taking her to bed, and that any woman should be proud and happy to accept the favor. They are not rapists, but one wonders what constrains them. Perhaps they too get headaches if they are deprived of sex for twelve hours. I mention men only because I know more men; sexual licentiousness is epicene. No doubt there are women who believe that any man should be proud and happy to accept their sexual favors, or that sex will get them anything from men. Both the men and the women of whom I speak assume that no one has any more inhibitions about sex than they have; they believe that pretended inhibitions about sex are hypocrisy. One wonders in what kind of home these men and women grew up; surely they did not develop the ethics of the bawdy house by the time they reached puberty without some adult help. There are other women who seem to have a deep conviction that all men with whom they deal, whatever their age, sex or condition, have only one thing in mind. When one meets such women one hopes the encounter will be brief.

I mention what may seem to be trivial traits of speech and behavior because they manifest a deep unthinking attitude toward sex which can be described as rape—or seduction, if one refuses the ugly word—by cultural pressure. How does one maintain any kind of principles, however loose, in a culture which constantly tells us that sex is inevitable, it is all around us, it is really just good clean sport, so why not relax and enjoy it? We walk and make children walk through the temple of Aphrodite. If the minds are stolen, one need not worry about the bodies; they will follow.

Whether it be accomplished by the violence of rape or the lies of seduction or the persuasion of the salesman, the free use of sex is not accomplished without the exploitation of persons, whether innocent or not, to serve the pleasure or profit of others; and the excuse has always been and will always be that they want it anyway. In a word, no one is going to be happy unless they are like me. I said above that the sex industry is all of one piece, and there is only one word for those who engage in it.

I have read and been told that sex is a wordless language of the deepest love which can arise between persons. This is why, as I noted earlier, the writer of Ephesians makes it the wordless language of the love of God. There has long been a feeling that the man and woman to whom this happens are lucky people—blessed, in the biblical phrase. One knows that there is nothing deep about the casual sex encounter of two consenting adults. One sees the desperate reaching out of two vacuities for something to fill their emptiness. A world which has forgotten how to love cannot manage its homes and rear its children or feed its hungry or sustain its needy or comfort its afflicted. Of such a world not the computer but the thermonuclear bomb may be the perfect symbol and the supreme achievement.

Chapter Seven

SEXUAL MORALITY
Part III

BEFORE I can lay aside the messy topic of sexual morality, there is some unfinished business which I simply cannot ignore, much as I would prefer to ignore it; it has probably become evident from my treatment that I find the entire topic distasteful. But since I have taken it up; I may as well take up all of it. One reason for not taking up the next two topics could be that contemporary discussion has turned them into legal issues rather than moral issues. As a citizen and a voter, I have a right to hold and to express my personal opinions on legal issues; but I cannot claim the competence which I think I can claim in theological issues. But the assertion that these issues are legal does not destroy their moral character. When I take up the discussion of abortion and homosexual relations I will find it difficult to keep the discussion on a moral level detached from convictions (or prejudices?) which I have held for many years. I shall try; cool rationality plays almost no part in the current discussion of these topics. Instead of a rational discussion, we are invited to join a parade. Parades bore me as much as rational discussion seems to bore many others; so if you do not mind, I will try to do my thing.

About abortion let it be said at once that the Bible says nothing about it from one end to the other. This does not mean that it is not a live moral problem; it means that, like other problems of moral life, it must be solved by the Christian wisdom of believers—for themselves, I should add, and for as many others as they can convince of the essential rationality and humanity of their attitude. The history of abortion in biblical times is not my concern; those who wish to know more should consult John Noonan's thorough study of the question. What may be of interest is the silence of the Bible on the common method of birth control practiced in the Roman world, especially by the poor; this was the exposure of unwanted infants to die from starvation and exposure. I imagine most students of ancient records still remember the chill and horror they felt when they read the letter of an Egyptian peasant, I think from the second or third century A.D., in which he tells his pregnant wife: if it is a boy, keep it; if it is a girl, expose it. And there is nothing antiquated about the practice. But the New Testament ignores it; and I would guess that even the most advanced right-to-choice advocates would find no moral ambiguity in infant exposure.

Yet one wonders why the right to choice should not be extended to include infanticide. We are, after all, dealing with the children of those who say they are nearly destitute; these children have an excellent chance of growing up diseased, stunted, deprived of education and opportunities, likely prospects for a short life of crime and depravity, doomed to be a burden to themselves and to society. The infant is only a potential human being, if humanity is to be measured by the quality of life and not merely by an unreal metaphysical definition. And surely the mothers of such unwanted and unloved children are as much entitled to emancipation as their more fortunate sisters to whom a more affluent culture or level of income affords opportunities for clean antiseptic abortion. I am not arguing this case, I am just exploring possibilities. It seems to me that if a case can be made for abortion, the same case can be made in the same circumstances for infanticide. Most people even into the twentieth century have found the classification of an infant as a person unreal. I recognize that infanticide is against the law, but laws can be changed to suit social changes and social needs. The same reasons which are adduced for euthanasia of the aged or hopelessly ill are valid for the unwanted infant, whose case is surely hopeless if those responsible for the gift of its life are unwilling to accept the burden of sustaining it. And let us not confuse the discussion by introducing moral issues.

One of the reasons why I am unwilling to discuss abortion is that it has been made clear to me that it is none of my business. My maleness makes it impossible for me to share the experience of pregnancy and parturition, and my sacerdotal state excludes me from personal concern in the problems of pregnant women. I believe the slogan is that I should keep my laws off their bodies. I cannot tell how earnestly I wish to maintain a total unconcern with the problems of abortion. I would like to keep my laws and my hands off women's bodies; they are not my laws, anyway. But somehow I got on the mailing list of a Ms. Eleanor Smeal, who signs herself Ellie. Ellie tells me that in spite of all I have heard it ought to be my business, and that all sorts of dire threats are impending, none of which touch me, and which her organization needs my money to avert. Well, Ellie, either it is my business or it is not. If you want some money from me (just call me Jack), I shall preserve my God-given choice on how to spend it; and you may as well know that I will not contribute a nickel for abortion. Call this narrow, call it cruel and unfeeling, call it anything as long as you call it my business; just keep your laws off my wallet. Since I left the Jesuits I became a taxpayer, an experience which I had never had. It makes one sharply aware of where public money is spent. This awareness, I feel, is not always shared by advocates of tax-supported causes. I will say simply that public funds for abortion hit me the same way that public funds for parochial schools hit other people. Those who have a blind spot for parochial schools should be able to understand me; but they probably will not.

I know that the law as interpreted by the courts takes away

my—God-given?—right of choice not to contribute to abortion, which might cast some doubt on whether God gave it. That legal decision is the result of no small amount of concerted agitation and propaganda; in a democratic society these are legitimate means of bringing to pass laws and legal decisions which say what you wish them to say. I trust that the same freedom of agitation and propaganda will be granted to those who try to change laws and legal decisions which do not say what they wish them to say. It is rather impressive how people, once they have achieved their desired legislation (or court decision), mouth piously, "It is the law of the land," as if it were the laws of the Medes and the Persians, when in fact it is an expression of the popular will at the time or it is nothing, reversible by the same processes by which it was formed. As I shall set forth shortly, I will not engage in agitation or propaganda (and thus I risk offending the American hierarchy). But it is so plainly absurd to deny that the processes which made abortion on demand legal cannot be reversed that one has to wonder whether one has not been transported suddenly from the United States to the Land of Oz. Popular sovereignty is not infallible; you cannot in the long run trust the people to do the right thing. They have too long a history of doing the wrong thing.

Society does, of course, inject law and the courts into moral decisions—or does it really? Perhaps, if we look closely, we shall find that laws leave strictly moral problems just where they were. We have laws against murder and theft; but what is murder, and what is theft? For reasons which would take us far beyond our present discussion, contemporary society shows a tolerance for murder which has made the incidence of murder in at least some parts of the United States the highest in known human history. Ineffective laws against murder and theft manifest a moral weakness of will in the society. I do not wish to wander too far afield, but merely to show that the moral force of law is much less than is thought. I cannot accept the belief of those who say that a society which has laws against murder should have laws against abortion. Laws must express a common consent, and ever since the question was first raised there has never been a common consent that abortion is murder in the legal sense of the term. And that is both the strength and the weakness of law, that it does not exceed the moral will of society. If written more strictly than that moral will, it will not be enforced. Hence I will not engage in agitation or propaganda for a constitutional amendment, because that is to put my trust in the same popular will which gave us abortion on demand, and makes me pay for it, in spite of a profound—I cannot tell you how profound—moral loathing for it.

I am afraid that by allowing abortion to become a legal issue we shall find ourselves excluded from discussing the moral issue. Modern Catholics have not found an effective way to present the moral issue of abortion to those who do not share their religion. Many statements against abortion have to be recognized as exaggerated; on an issue as sensitive as this, such statements lose ground. It is not arguments we wish to win, but people. I confess that I have not found the message either; my masculine and celibate detachment previously mentioned makes me an unlikely messenger; we need to hear from those who are personally concerned. If I must treat the topic, I see nothing better for me to do than to return to what I have said in these essays earlier; sex must be recognized as the most intimate of interpersonal relationships which must be entered responsibly. Those who have known and cherished deep friendship know that it is not an exploitation of a friend, it is not entered casually, it both generates and fosters deep personal understanding and consideration, it is precious enough to be preserved at the cost of some personal pride, and its rupture is an unthinkable disaster. It is an old saying that you can choose your friends, but you are stuck with your relatives. Certainly a true friendship would never be shattered by a new infatuation. All this suggests that people show more maturity and responsibility in forming and retaining friendship than they do in forming sexual relations; or perhaps those who are incapable of one are incapable of both. I will not say that two who are genuinely and deeply in love would never have the need for an abortion; I do know that for such we need not legislate.

The mention of friendship leads me to my second piece of unfinished business, which I take up with even more distaste than abortion; I mean the rather warm issue of homosexuality. At my age one would be expected to follow the old rule; let it not be even mentioned among us. Let me say again that the Bible says nothing about it. The few references are casual and random. They are also quite abusive, as popular language has always been. If one wanted to argue that these texts (like most texts on the position of women) reflect no more than the cultural patterns of the time, and that popular language here is as valid as popular language on astronomy, I would not dispute it. After all, the Bible condemns witches to death, and we no longer do that—not because we think they are without malice, but we are sure their malice is ineffective. If they commit a crime under civil law, it can only be fraud.

In the world of the ancient Near East, in which the Old Testament was written, homosexuality seems to have had a bad reputation. Thus the few biblical references to it may reflect no more than a cultural pattern not limited to ancient Israel. This does not mean that they reflect nothing. The Greeks of the most creative century of Greek history exhibited a quite different cultural pattern. The love of which Plato wrote with so much sensitivity in the *Symposium* is not the love of man and woman, but the love of man and boy, for which the Greeks had a word. The Greeks were also the cultural heirs of such masculine heroes as Achilles and Ajax, and earlier Greek times reflect the ancient Near Eastern attitude rather than the classical attitude. In any case, there is no doubt that cultural patterns, which we have seen more than once are effective moral determinants, have not been uniform towards homosexuality. I said earlier that one flouts them at one's peril. The Romans of the Republic, who would probably have been quite at home spiritually with the soldiers of Cromwell's New Model Army, had unflattering words for the homosexual; the most polite Latin term is translated as soft. The more tolerant Greeks commonly used a word which decency forbids me to translate. Apparently few Greeks were as sophisticated as Plato, which one knew already.

The modern movement for Gay Liberation seems to be intended to alter some long-standing cultural patterns. I probably would flatter its proponents by supposing that they intend to alter moral standards. I am not sure that many of my contemporaries attach any meaning to the words moral standards. Whether they intend the one or the other, they certainly have their work cut out for them. They should not be surprised, and probably are not, at the magnitude of the task they have set themselves. It does occur to me that they too fall into the error of thinking that a few changes in law and a few favorable court decisions will take care of their problem. I repeat what I wrote above: unless a law is an expression of the popular will of the time, it is nothing.

Since the problem is by no means new, it will probably not go away quickly, and it seems that we shall have to live with it. It appears that more than anything else what is needed is a large dose of old-fashioned charity. We were taught as children that no one should be excluded from the scope of charity, and we spend the rest of our lives learning what it means. Gay people, to use the designation which they prefer, should not exclude straight people, nor should straight people exclude gays. Modern studies may show something which has never been shown before, that homosexuality and not heterosexuality is natural for some individuals; I doubt this, but I admit that my mind was closed on the subject some years ago. I am trained, however, to keep an open mind where possible. I have not had enough training to think that the "affair," in the usual sense of the word, is morally more tolerable if it is homosexual than if it is heterosexual. Society is unwilling to treat the homosexual encounter as anything but an affair. Perhaps some Christian charity is required to understand how difficult it is to keep an open mind when so many years of habits of thought—prejudice, if you will—block the opening.

If it should be established that homosexuality creates a third sex, admitting the fact will not solve the problem. Homosexuals have survived by going underground. They seem no longer willing to hide. One has to respond to this necessity imposed by society the same way one responds to racial segregation; ultimately it is cruel and inhuman and must be renounced. We have learned that to say we renounce it does not create a genuinely integrated society, and that cruelty may be done by forcing integration. The law can halt open and obvious injustice done to others because of what society thinks is deviant, whether it be race, sexual conduct, poverty, or crime. The law cannot correct the social judgment which lies at the root of cruelty and makes some degree of cruelty socially acceptable. Such a change in social attitudes, we believe, is the objective of the saving event which God wrought in Jesus Christ; it implies a change in the character of the individual members of society, and nothing less.

I suppose one of the most obvious and now tedious lessons which we think Jesus taught us is that we should not make enemies, but treat enemies as friends. One does not make friends by insisting on one's claims, but by recognizing that others have claims too. Whether homosexuality be a vice, as most of society has long thought, or a disease, which some experts think, or a variant form of normal behavior, as homosexuals now urge, nothing will change if homosexuals and heterosexuals meet only in hostile confrontation, each urging their sacred rights and treating the others as non-people. This is not much of a solution; but until a genuine Christian approach is made by both sides, no humane solution is possible.

Hence, without any further information beyond a general character, I must be sympathetic to a recently formed ministry to homosexuals. I realize that such a ministry is open to many risks; but that has been true of all specialized ministries to those whom society has rejected. I am antecedently well disposed because the ministry to such is in character with the Jesus of history, if there is a Jesus of history. The place where I have difficulty placing the Jesus of history in imagination is in the lobbies of legislative chambers. The only time he went near what came close to one in his day he got killed. Reconciliation, not legislation, is his business. I should think his followers would want to make it their skill.

By way of summary and conclusion to these scattered remarks on sexual morality I shall adduce a biblical passage which is not brought up in this connection in contemporary interpretation, although it was often brought up in the interpretation of past ages. This is the story of Adam and Eve in the garden of Eden, for centuries in Christian interpretation understood as the story of the fall of man from grace. As early at least as the Church Father Irenaeus in the second century —I am working from my unaided memory—some understood the man and woman in Eden to be two children with the sexual innocence of children. The tempter is the devil; the fruit offered the two, "sweet to eat and fair to look upon," was the union of sex. The original sin into which man fell was the discovery of sex, and his fall was growing up from innocence to maturity; in fact it was growth into puberty. This interpretation of the story has always exercised an attraction for readers, especially for those who fancied themselves poets, and it has never disappeared from popular speech. Interpreters find it theologically unsound for more reasons than I can set forth here—I with others have set them forth elsewhere—but modern interpreters recognize the presence of sexual motifs in the story; and they believe these must be taken into account in grasping what the author was trying to say.

The interpretation thus briefly set forth may be theologically unsound, but it seems to anticipate the contemporary attitude towards sex rather well. Unlimited sexual freedom is now seen by many as the full maturity of humankind, not a fall from grace but a rise to new heights; in the biblical phrase, you shall be like gods, knowing—that is, masters of good and evil. Once these taboos are overcome there is no challenge too great, no achievement you may not dare, no success beyond your hopes. You shall achieve what an unenlightened poet denied you; your grasp shall equal your reach. The only thing wrong with man is that he has not yet grown up. Our contemporaries are convinced that this growth is as necessary and as inevitable as the growth of the individual from childhood and innocence to maturity and understanding. Those who attempt to inhibit this growth are trying to do to mankind at large what the Chinese once did to the feet of small girls.

Is this popular belief mythology too? Mythology is neither demonstrated nor refuted by logic or science. The biblical wise man concluded his story by adding that the only thing the man and the woman discovered was that they were naked. I am impressed by the fact that the promised new freedom has furnished so much material for Father Bruce Ritter's mission in New York. Perhaps I should weigh this against other things. I would just like to know what they are. It is true that the price of maturation is that the simple joys and happiness of childhood must be renounced. They are renounced because maturity offers far deeper joys and happiness; and the adult who looks back with genuine longing on his or her childhood is in serious trouble. Is the new sexual freedom a dream of a perpetually irresponsible childhood, unclouded by adult responsibilities?

In the opinion of some interpreters, the biblical wise man told his story in opposition to the ancient cult of fertility, which deified sex in a way which even modern pornographers would find remarkable, if they ever read about it. In this religion sex was life, sex gave everything, and while it did not promise immortality it promised to make death tolerable. It did not, of course; I spoke earlier of the profound pessimism of ancient man in the face of death. I think the modern world has hauled the cult of fertility out of the dustbin of history and presented it as a new world of promise. If Ishtar were surviving, she would laugh herself sick at this concourse of new worshipers.

Chapter Eight

THE HEREAFTER

IN an earlier chapter I discussed death. A correspondent wrote that he was astonished that a student of both Testaments who had spent his life in a restricted clerical and monastic mode of life should declare that he sometimes was not sure that he believed in another life after death. The correspondent knew me in my earlier years; and he should have remembered that the life was not monastic. The Jesuits are not monks. With that reservation, I do not see why a restricted and regular religious life should prevent a man from experiencing a doubt commonly experienced by many; the life does not prevent him from having temptations. A study of both Testaments does indeed, after some time, possibly deepen one's faith in another life; but certainly many who have studied them long and deeply have found that their studies issued in agnosticism. It is quite true that many of those who govern the clerical and restricted life of religious have done their best either to suppress or, failing that, to channel the thinking of the members; but these efforts have not been uniformly successful. I observed to my correspondent that anyone who said that a doubt about the future life never crossed his or her mind could most kindly be said never to have given the problem any thought. I believe that I do not scandalize adult readers by telling them that their problems are shared by others.

Your friends who say that they do not or cannot believe in a future life may take a position which is extreme or irreverent or discourteous; but it is not absurd, and you should not tell them it is. If they say they are sure we die like dogs (as an uncle of mine used to say—now, I hope, not dead like a dog), you may safely tell them you are not as sure as they are that there is no difference between my life and the life of a dog, and that this affords at least a question whether our deaths are alike. If they say they simply do not know, they take an irrefutable position; there is nothing you can add to their knowledge. You can only present your motives for believing and hoping that life does not end with death; and you must admit that your motives for this belief and hope are not rational. You may add that most of your beliefs and hopes, like theirs, do not rest on purely rational motives. And there perhaps you must let the matter drop. Much is required to found a belief and hope in the future life, much more than most believers have ever had to put into it. I will not say that they have never come face to face with evil; it is known that this encounter more often than not shatters the shallow faith and hope of most believers in God and the future life. One who survives this encounter really believes; knowing how he reached his belief, he does not think it can glibly be imposed on others.

I do not know what is now being taught children in catechetical instruction; like all Catholics of the older generations, I was reared in what I now know is the traditional mythology of judgment, purgatory, heaven and hell. I suppose some will find my use of the word mythology offensive; in this discussion, which is concerned with quite vital and ultimate issues, I cannot afford to let excessively delicate sensibilities prevent me from using quite accurate theological language. Myth is a way of thinking and talking about things which are believed to be realities, which lie entirely outside normal human experience and memory, collective or individual. Myth is normally imaginative and often poetically imaginative.

To say that something is mythical says nothing about the reality or the unreality of the topic; it says that the representation is couched in symbolic images, and one is asked to do no more than to learn the difference between the reality symbolized and its image. In foreign cultures this may be quite difficult. But myth is neither true nor false by definition anymore than philosophy or science is. All three may be vehicles of truth, and all three may be vehicles of error, deception and lies. But one must go outside the particular world of discourse or of image to verify the truth of what is expressed. All this was perhaps necessary to say that when we were reared in the mythology of the afterlife we were not being reared in a tissue of falsehood; we were being taught in the language of image and symbol, sometimes more aptly and sometimes less, to apprehend some truths which in later life, after some years of philosophical reading and reflection, I cherish more rather than less. I did not cease to believe that my parents were real when I discovered that Santa Claus, who is quite unreal, was "really" my parents.

My problem in this exposition is that I do not know how to vest the truths expressed by traditional mythology in a form attractive and convincing to those for whom judgment, heaven and hell have become as real as Santa Claus. The temptation is to resort to the abstract language of philosophical thought, which I have learned to like because, well used, it makes possible a clarity and precision which are achieved in no other way. I know that this is an acquired taste not shared by everyone; and someone will ask, why not leave them with Santa Claus? Because educated adults will recognize what you are doing and will withdraw their attention as rapidly as they politely can. They will think, more correctly than you realize, that you do not take them or the problem seriously.

At the risk of further confusing an already confused question, it must be stated that belief in survival or an afterlife is not identical with belief in the immortality of the soul. The immortality of the soul is a philosophical idea which we have learned from the ancient Greeks; Plato represents Socrates as giving eloquent and moving expression to this belief the night of his death. The immortality of the soul is not a biblical idea. The Hebrew and Greek words often translated "soul" do not at all carry in the original languages of the biblical books the meaning, vague as it is, carried by the English word "soul." The belief in survival after death is expressed in the Bible as a belief in the resurrection of the body. Both ideas are quite difficult; they are in fact efforts to imagine what survival would be like, and they fail because they imagine it in terms of a restoration or a continuation of the present life of experience. To say that one believes in survival is to affirm that one believes in something which cannot be described in terms of experience; and that is precisely what we said the objects of myth are. Hence belief in immortality is belief in a more sophisticated myth, and belief in resurrection is belief in a less sophisticated myth. This, to repeat, is to say that they are symbols; to affirm that there is a reality which they symbolize is a further step.

Hence I do not question the reality of the afterlife when I point out that the immortality of the soul fails to represent the survival of the human person. We are animals, not souls; as animals we die, and an afterlife, if it is to be ours, must be the afterlife of an animal. Otherwise, it is not we but someone else who survives. Belief in the resurrection of the body is in this respect a more satisfying myth. It also fails because it is impossible to think of it except as a return to the life ended by death; as such, it comes perilously close to a contradiction in terms. Paul recognized this when he attacked the problem in his first letter to the Corinthians (chapter 15). There he says that flesh and blood cannot possess the kingdom of God; hence what dies is a "natural body," what rises is a "spiritual body.'' And what is a spiritual body? Paul did not say because he did not know. Myth is necessary, but it has its limitations.

Yet each of us is faced with the fact of daily experience that the life we have is not shared with any other type of living creature in the universe of our experience. Whatever science may tell us, there are difficulties in believing that all animals die in the same way. A promise based on our religious faith meets a receptive audience, in spite of the difficulties in believing and the impossibility of understanding it. There are also serious, some would say insuperable, difficulties in believing, in the phrase of my late uncle, that we die like dogs. If so, why do we not live like dogs? It may be urged that Christian faith in the afterlife is of a piece with all beliefs in an afterlife; that they all respose on man's native unwillingness to die. Those who do not ask themselves why man is the only animal that knows it is going to die find that this unwillingness explains everything; they have no further problems beyond the problem of life itself. Apparently it does not bother them that life makes no sense.

A biblical poet, the author of the book of Job, thus stated the problem of life (3:20-22):

> Why is light given to the toilers, and life to the bitter of spirit?
> They wait for death and it comes not; they search for it rather than for hidden treasures,
> Rejoice in it exultingly, and are glad when they reach the grave.

Mankind has been endowed with a reach which exceeds his grasp, to borrow a phrase, and any faith in God demands that this should not be a diabolical cosmic prank. If one does not believe in God, one must believe in a devil. Christian mythology of the afterlife has found ways of representing how mankind can achieve the fulfillment for which he strives in spite of the fact that experience shows that fulfillment is achieved rarely and only for a few; I will concede that these few, as far as we can observe, have no need of survival. But it must be admitted that mankind by the millions die as meaningfully as fruit-flies. Christianity proclaims that Jesus Christ is their savior too.

Christian belief is that each human person can reach a fulfilled life; that God has made this possible through Jesus Christ; and that the fulfillment is enduring. It affirms also that man's will for fulfillment is not as stable or as persevering as his desire for fulfillment, but that the gift of God can be accepted if man so chooses. This puts it much more abstractly and much less realistically than the traditional mythology; but perhaps those who find the traditional myths incredible will find another myth more to their tastes. Man's deepest and personal needs, arising from some inner source which cannot be suppressed, are components of reality too, and not to be dismissed as unreal simply because they are immensurable—or inexplicable. I have learned to believe that the God who is responsible for something instead of nothing, for the existence of life at all rather than inert matter, is also able and willing to bring that life to the fulfillment which it demands; and this is no more of an intellectual problem than understanding why there should be something rather than nothing.

The myth of heaven was an attempt to express the human hope and desire for complete fulfillment of human potentialities. Believers accept the implication that this fulfillment must ultimately be a gift of God; agnostics believe—with no more foundation in reality—that it can be achieved by the human will. But what are the potentalities of the human being? That there are and must be limits seems self-evident; but we cannot define them. Experience seems to tell us that man may not do all that he can do. I referred earlier to a theme of

classical Greek tragedy which sees human success as ultimately self-defeating. Man ruins himself by his very achievements;
there is no tragedy about man ruining himself by refusing to
achieve, because that would not be good theater. But the visible potentialities of mankind are awesome. To take some
pedestrian examples: the seventeen-foot pole vault and the
four-minute mile were for centuries regarded as physically
impossible. The amount of physical punishment which the
human being, properly trained and conditioned, can absorb
in a professional football or basketball game would have
been incredible even earlier in this century.

The human mind has wrought achievements within the last
century which would have been thought divine or diabolical
achievements in earlier centuries. The wonders—and we no
longer use the word—of the computer, jet travel and now
space travel and thermonuclear power have become routine.
Even more wonderful is the fact that these achievements have
been done by a race whose level of morality has not evolved
beyond that of the Stone Age, whose proudest technical
achievements have been done in the same century with the
two World Wars and the Holocaust. These remind us that the
awesome potentialities of humanity can turn to evil as well as
to good. Heaven is a dream that these potentialities will be
entirely turned to good.

The myth of heaven recognizes that the fulfillment of
human potential is the finding of God, that it cannot be
achieved unless man seeks it in God (that is to say, outside of
himself), that the fulfillment is the will and the gift of God.
The myth has made this hope real for countless believers who
could not grasp abstractions, in spite of the fact that, like
many myths, it has often been mixed with errors, some of
which were pernicious. Many forms of the myth tell us more
about the believers than they do about the reality symbolized
by the image. The ancient Islamic and thoroughly masculine

heaven of an unlimited harem could easily be shared by many of my contemporaries in modern Europe and America. It tells us what these believers think human fulfillment is, but not much about what human fulfillment really might be. Many forms of belief in heaven have been adult versions of a great rock candy mountain. The same must be said of many forms of the modern myth of progress, which has become the myth of heaven for a post-Christian age. But if children only want heaven to be a great mountain of rock candy and ice cream, they will not be thrilled by a heaven which is the music of an eternal symphony with never a false note—nor will those who want the unlimited harem. If one believes in any kind of heaven, one believes not only that God can surprise us (already said by Paul quoting Isaiah), but that we can surprise ourselves by discovering what human beings can be when they reach their fullness; like gods, an ancient biblical myth said. This is not merely the satisfaction of all their desires.

Corresponding to the myth of heaven as the fulfillment of human potentialities, there is the myth of hell as the myth of total human failure. This myth modern man rejects; and perhaps it deserves some thought. Are we not a bit like children who think that toys and windows are unbreakable, that pets are immortal, that fire does not burn, that there is no hurt which will not be healed by mommy's kiss? Does God really take human life and well-being as seriously as we know, deep down, that we ought to take it? Even the most sophisticated unbeliever rejects the idea that Hitler was just a boyish prankster; yet this is what the modern myth of total irresponsibility comes to. It will be said that we have to draw the line somewhere, and I agree; ultimately that is all the myth of hell was trying to say, and all I am trying to say. Or does modern man think that human freedom is a myth and a delusion too? If it is not, then we must accept the human capacity of self-destruction. And that is hell, with or without eternal fire.

Some people say that they cannot combine belief in God whose mercy is above all his works with a belief in hell or eternal damnation. I will be honest and say that the combination gives me trouble too. But until someone convinces me that human malice and the harm it does are imaginary objects, I have to say that a world in which these things are morally as good as their opposites gives me trouble too. No doubt the mercy of God finds ways of doing things of which I am ignorant, and I am willing to trust myself to it; but wisdom from some very excellent sources warns me against presuming on it. To say that human malice and its consequences are nothing in the ultimate account is to say that Jesus died for nothing in the ultimate account. I do not think my profession permits me to utter that kind of blasphemy.

So I have trouble with the myth of hell, and I have more trouble if I deny the mysterious reality of which the myth of hell is possibly a clumsy expression. Those who think it is may ask themselves whether any modern writer has expressed as well his belief in the myth of the essential goodness of man or the myth of total irresponsibility as Dante expressed his belief in the myths of hell, purgatory and heaven. I observed that even the most sophisticated agnostic might find room in hell for Hitler and a few other moral monsters. But this is to treat as inconsequential the neighborhood bully, the block gossip, the office tyrant, the village skinflint, the street mugger, and the innumerable other petty Hitler's whose malice is limited only by their scope of operations—village Cromwells, guiltless of their country's blood only because fortune—or a kindly providence—denied them the opportunities. They, and all of us, make life hell for each other.

So perhaps the ultimate myth of the afterlife, the myth which both raises and answers all questions, is not the myth of heaven or the myth of hell, but the myth of judgment. The myth of judgment states—and leave the quite imaginary valley of Jehoshaphat out of it—that God does hold us human beings accountable for our actions. It is the ultimate denial of the myth of total irresponsibility, of the myth of essential human goodness, of the happy belief that we are all just good little people, perhaps childishly playful, but so lovable and forgivable. It can be a terrifying thought that we have to pay for our fun, that there is no free lunch in this life or the next. It is so terrifying that many find it unthinkable and unutterable. But consider: if there is a hell, I cannot think of anything more horrible than survival in a human company whose members had achieved total irresponsibility, had become unloving and uncaring, who owed no one anything, who needed no one nor were needed by anyone. The myth of judgment says that God finds such a state of humanity intolerable.

A friend and colleague (now deceased), a professor at Yale, once in an address to a group of his colleagues pointed out the paradox he had noticed in two then recent utterances of Mr. Khrushchev and Mr. John Kennedy. Mr. Khrushchev, the professed atheist, had used the phrase "as God sees me." Mr. Kennedy, the devout Catholic, had referred to "history as the sole judge of our actions and a good conscience as our only reward." The only point I wish to make of the anecdote is that the phrase of Mr. Kennedy is just as mythological as the phrase of Mr. Khrushchev; and I suppose I should be happy that I, like them, have available a set of ready cant phrases with which I can mask my real beliefs, if I have any, or my lack of beliefs, if there is nothing there. And perhaps I may even fool myself into not seeing that behind the ready phrases there lurks a very frightened man.

I have said nothing about the old Roman Catholic myth of purgatory. Since the end of the Second Vatican Council the church no longer imposes this belief on its members. I think I may regard it as an effort to express in myth the belief that somehow a merciful God will bail us out of the scrapes into which our own wickedness and folly have got us. As such it is worth preserving in some form. The old-fashioned simple faith liked such stories as that of the apparition of the departed soul who said, "Between the bridge and the stream I found mercy." It is quite true that the mercy of God cannot be exaggerated. It should be added that neither, like his justice, can it be understood nor rationalized. Both are best worshiped in silence.

Chapter Nine

VIOLENCE AND THE KINGDOM

AN obscure saying of Jesus which is preserved both in Matthew (11:12) and Luke (16:16) speaks of the kingdom of heaven as the object of violence. The saying (probably derived from a common source) is considerably watered down in Luke to the point where it becomes nearly unintelligible; either Luke did not understand the saying or thought it too harsh to repeat as he found it. Since it is almost the only saying of Jesus which touches on the topic of violence, it is no wonder that it is obscure. The advice given in Luke 22:35-38 to buy a purse and a sword, reversing the recommendations given for the apostolic mission, is also obscure. A recent writer (Stuhlmueller) has said: "Practically all commentators take the reference to purse, wallet and sword figuratively. The disciples must be ready for any and every circumstance." Let us say now—for we shall pursue this topic below—that any alleged recommendations of violence in the sayings of Jesus are at least much less clear than, for example, the recommendations to love one's neighbor and to forgive one's enemies.

I have been asked to comment upon the theology of liberation; if this request sends me at once to the response of the Gospels to violence, it should be evident why. If my own response shows a misconception of liberation theology, I have to answer that my response has been largely formed by those who seek my support; apparently they think that their propaganda is all I need to know. There is a considerable literature on liberation theology; I reviewed one book on the subject, and my review was not favorable. But most of those to whom appeals for support are made are not asked to read even one book; they are asked to embrace a cause. The cause

107

is the liberation of the poor from oppression, and it is presented as a rather clear choice between standing where Jesus stood, with the poor and against the oppressors, or on the side of the oppressors. But I have not embraced causes uncritically for forty years; frankly, the proponents of liberation theology ask from me the kind of total support which I do not give even to the Roman Catholic Church, for which I guess I would, with some grumbling, probably die. After all, I must die sometime, and the Roman Catholic Church, in spite of some numerous and fairly obvious flaws, is at least as good a cause for which to die as any other. Perhaps I had better state why the cause of liberation cannot claim that identity with Jesus and the church which would entitle it to the same total loyalty.

Let me first make a personal statement which others need not accept and may not even like. I said I would probably die for the church, and I mean it. I will not accept the claims of any churchman, including the chief, to tell me how to think. I am thoroughly convinced that Jesus never made that claim and that no one can with any shred of veracity make that claim on his behalf. This, as I hear liberation theologians, is exactly the claim that they make. Those who discuss or question any of their theses are dismissed as capitalist swine. I am sorry, but you can have my total loyalty only at the cost of letting me talk. There are enough intellectual bullies in the world already, and I see no reason for lifting a finger or a dime to support more. If I have misunderstood the attitude of liberation theologians towards free discussion, which is my living, it is time for them to say so.

So far, then, you have my personal considerations; those who can share them may do so, those who feel unconcerned are free to ignore them. The other questions which I have to raise have a broader interest. The first question is this: does liberation theology invite me to engage in a war, and indeed, in a class war, the ugliest kind of strife known, where humanity most quickly and surely becomes inhuman? Perhaps that is not the meaning of the invitation; but unless I am totally bereft of my wits, my mail and certain publications contain invitations to watch over the garments of those who throw the stones, to put it mildly. These are invitations to support political activities with purposes which cannot be realistically achieved without violence, and a violence which will be carried on without quarter until the extermination of the enemies. Possibly what I ask is no more than a moderation of rhetoric. Revolutions have always fed upon inflated rhetoric. If one reads the rhetoric of the rebellious colonies of North America in 1776, one would never suspect that the rebellion was coalition of oligarchs, the slave traders and the rumrunners of Boston and the slaveowning planters of Virginia. These wealthy middle-class gentlemen were hardly those whose claims were being forged on the plains of Boston. I am not suggesting an analogy, merely pointing out that one learns to be skeptical about revolutionary rhetoric. It all sounds very much alike; and if it can make George Washington and John Adams victims of an oppressive tyrant, it could sell refrigerators to Eskimos.

But even if the revolutionary rhetoric is properly discounted, will there remain enough to establish a good cause, as worthy of my support as other causes which are proposed to me? I will not dispute that Jesus was on the side of the poor—and he was poor by rearing, not by an adopted career. (I shall devote the next chapter of this book to the attitude of the New Testament toward wealth and poverty.) But I am not asked to support a good cause; I am asked to support a war. Over the years I have convinced myself and a few others that I cannot, if I profess to be a Christian, support any war as a means to achieve any human objective, no matter how noble it may be. If the objectives of the liberation movement are not to be achieved by war, then they are to be achieved by political means. To this I must respond that Jesus neither engaged in politics nor ever recommended politics as a means of achieving whatever it was he wished to achieve; and his response to violence and to politics will occupy the rest of this chapter.

Probably most Bible readers do not know that Jesus had the option of armed resistance to what the majority of his countrymen thought, rightly or wrongly, was oppression. It seems that the number of Jews who regarded Rome as an oppressor was greater than the number of British colonists in North America who so regarded the rule of King and Parliament in 1776. There was no real hope of a successful rebellion; rebels have always been long on idealism, and with a very few exceptions, short on practical management—which may be more to their credit. The Jews who died hopelessly at Masada have become national symbols. The death of Jesus on Calvary was politically more hopeless. It has long seemed strange to me that Jesus should have been regarded as a mystic, an idealist, a dreamer, when these qualities could have been much more properly applied to many of his contemporaries; Jesus was a practical person in the sense that he proposed a program which anyone could follow.

Several years ago, an English scholar, the late S.G.F. Brandon, dedicated a few books to proving that Jesus was a Zealot, the name given to members of the radical and violent opposition to Rome, and that Roman justice made no mistake when it executed him as a bandit—the name the Romans gave to freedom fighters. Brandon argued from a few Gospel passages, most from the Gospel of John, and found that the crucifixion of Jesus was an elaborate plot intended to issue in an insurrection. The plot miscarried, and the women who went to the tomb found to their horror that he was near expiration. The disciples went ahead with the plot and a proclamation that he had risen. Brandon convinced almost none of our colleagues; yet, apart from the elaborate resurrection plot, he assembled about all the Gospel evidence to show that Jesus was really a Zealot. He was forced to postulate an even more elaborate conspiracy to transform a revolutionary into one who totally rejected violence. For that is the Jesus of the Gospels, and contemporary scholarship, except for liberation theology, does not argue the point.

I have trouble with the implication that our contemporary situation is so different that Jesus could say nothing relevant to it, that we can act in the spirit of Jesus only by doing things he did not do, refused to do, and said were alien to discipleship. I sometimes wonder whether modern liberation theologians and liberators are informed about the social and economic world of the Roman Empire. I shall discuss this more at length in the following essay; it will become clear, I hope, that the poor of the world of New Testament times were as desperately oppressed as the poor of large regions of South America and Asia. Let me illustrate. The celebrated *pax Romana,* the Roman peace, involved economic problems. The Romans ended war within their territory, their *imperium,* but they also took away the chief source of slaves, who were mostly captives of war. The island of Delos, which was as specialized a community as Zurich or Las Vegas, was the principal slave market of the Mediterranean; on a normal day it handled the sale of ten or twelve thousand slaves (if my memory serves me). Slavery was the destination of the poor who fell beneath the wheels of the economic juggernaut, if they survived. Some have thought it strange that the New Testament pays almost no attention to slavery. Why did not Jesus say, "Slaves of the world, unite! You have nothing to lose but your chains"? It would have been much more realistic if said by him. Instead he suggested ways in which even slaves could find fulfillment. If those ways are not good enough, let those who think so say it clearly.

To say that the poor whom Jesus called blessed were not really poor is to speak from ignorance; to say that we have found a better way to address the problem is to say that Jesus said or did nothing relevant to one of the most pressing human problems. To say that we must now approach the problem by declaring a class war in his name is to pick up the weapons he rejected. I am not thinking of the saying of Matthew 26:52: "Those who take up the sword will perish by the sword." I am not sure Jesus said this, and it may be a saying from an earlier Jewish collection of wisdom, added to the narrative by the evangelist under the (mistaken?) impression that it expressed the mind of Jesus. I am thinking of the solution to human problems which is expressed throughout the Gospels; this is the solution of reconciliation, of forgiveness of enemies. Jesus was a peacemaker, not like the Romans, of whom a Roman writer nearly contemporary with the Gospels wrote, "They make a desert and call it peace." It is obvious that anyone who follows the recommendations of Jesus will be the patsy of the human community in which he lives; I think it shows a low estimate of the intelligence of Jesus to say that he did not know it too. As I read the Gospels, I read that there is no salvation for humanity unless and until the patsies outnumber the fighters. Crude, perhaps, but not as crude nor as incredible as the image of Jesus with the machine gun. Jesus taught us how to die, not how to kill; and if he did not say that our salvation lies in death and not in killing, he did not say anything. John Wayne, not Jesus, should be our hero and our model.

I am supposed to conclude, it seems, that the clear teaching of Jesus is no longer any good because it does not work; the poor are still poor and the oppressors still oppress. I do not know what "working" in this context would mean. Apparently we are supposed to enrich the poor, which Jesus never promised. Apparently poverty, and not money, is the root of all evil. In any case I remember the answer of a well-known defender of the cause of liberation when I urged that the whole discussion had omitted the theme of reconciliation, which I thought was prominent in the Gospels: "We are willing to reconcile after we get what we want." I remember it because the answer put what reconciliation is not as briefly and as baldly as I ever heard it; and the speaker was minister of a Christian church. Peace among men is not what we really want; our own way is what we really want. In my lifetime "peace at any price" was a slogan of dishonor.

I fear that I am repeating what liberation theologians and many others before them have said is the hypocrisy of historic Christianity; tell the poor to bear their burdens patiently and God will reward them, while I tell the rich oppressors nothing. I know, and perhaps I should say, that the Catholic Church has been for centuries a kept church, the chaplains and spiritual lackeys of the rich and the powerful. It has not done its duty to proclaim to the wealthy as well as to the poor that they should sell all and give to the poor if they wish to enter the kingdom of heaven. It has not repeated Paul's directions to the Corinthians: where there is inequity, those who have more should bring equality to pass by sharing what they have with those who have less to the point where there is a sufficiency for all and superabundance for none. I shall, as I said above, dwell upon these elements of the New Testament attitude toward wealth in the next essay. But the church has this message to preach, and it has a mandate to preach it, I cannot find a mandate to preach strife and bloody revolution. It has always been difficult for the wealthy to see where the cross they must carry is to be found; but many Christians have found it, and the Catholic Church, in spite of its lackey position, has never lacked men and women with the courage to announce this message, and to tell Catholics that the ransom of their souls by the endowment of churches and colleges with rich vessels, vestments, buildings, ornamentation and libraries does less honor to God than feeding the hungry and clothing the naked whom Jesus identified with himself. That the church has not always, or perhaps not even often proclaimed this gospel is hardly a reason to declare that the gospel is a failure, and that instead of the gospel it is time to summon every man and woman to the barricades.

Possibly I exaggerate the violent implications of liberation theology; it would not surprise me if I were told so. Possibly we are asked to support not gunrunning but political action. And this is an option which Jesus did not have and therefore could not refuse. Political action was simply not within the horizon of his possibilities. Democratic processes are a development of modern times, like electricity and the steam engine and the other blessings of the Industrial Revolution. Would Jesus have refused to use the techniques of the industrial age? And is it not just as narrow to restrict Christians to the political techniques of the Augustan age? Is that not archaism? I have to say that I do not know; it is a chancy thing (and I do it often enough myself to know) to determine what Jesus would have said or done in situations which he never encountered. Yet this is the sort of chancy decision which the Christian must make daily about his life in a world quite different from the world of Palestine of the first century. However, if he is a Christian, he believes he will find in the New Testament materials from which he can form his decision; and he is willing to make the chancy decision, hoping that any mistakes he makes will be Christian. Hence I will say: the Roman world furnished much more ample resources to do what Jesus did—admitting that we have not yet learned what it really was that he did—than Jesus employed. If he chose his means in modern times with the same parsimony which he exhibited in the first century, he would have, for example,

none of the resources which I have had for teaching and
writing for forty years—and I never thought I had enough.
So much for the techniques of the Industrial Revolution—or
of modern research, or of modern public relations, or of any
kind of prestige. Of what passed for prestige in the world in
which he lived he had none. We who need so much more to
do what little we do have never weighed the implications of
the saying, "Provide yourselves with neither gold nor silver
nor copper in your belts; no traveling bag, no change of shirt,
no sandals, no walking staff" (Matthew 10:9-10, *New American Bible)*.

I will admit that Jesus gave no instructions on how to become involved in politics and how to employ them as means
for his purposes. That leaves me, I think, much in the same
position as the fact that Jesus left me no instructions on how
to invest my savings (of which I have a meager amount) or
how to engage in university education (which I have done).
To say that there is no Christian way of doing these things
may be to say too much; I am uneasy with the clear implication of the Gospels that I should have no problem in investing
savings because I should not have any or the equally clear implications of the value of human wisdom—it has none. But
they are not clearly wrong. At the same time, it is futile to
look in the Gospels for a Christian way to amass wealth. Is it
equally futile to look there for a Christian way to amass
power? But I can do so much good with wealth if I use it
rightly; so can I do so much good with power if I use it rightly. And since this was as true in the first century as it is now,
why could not Jesus have spared a few words for those who
yield so much power and influence in the world rather than
leave us with the impression that there is no "right" or Christian way to use power or wealth, just as there is no right or
Christian way to use violence?

For three hundred years the church had no problem of how

to be involved in politics except the problem of survival. Then Constantine became a Christian, Rome became Christian, and the Catholic Church became Roman. Viewed from a distance of seventeen hundred years, it was a doubtful blessing. I do not think any historian or theologian would seriously maintain any longer that the union of church and state is the ideal condition or that it has ever been good for either church or state; and certainly no one shows any desire to restore it. It can be seriously asserted that political means have never been effective in the mission of the church, and that the instances in which their use has not been harmful to that mission are rare indeed. When I am now told that one more time and we will do it so right that it will never have to be done again, I think I hear a confirmed drunk telling me that just one more fling at the bottle will be enough.

There is one saying of Jesus which touches on political involvement, though not very directly; that is the saying of Mark 10:42-44, paralleled in Matthew and Luke: "You know how among the Gentiles those who seem to exercise authority lord it over them; their great ones make their importance felt. It cannot be like that with you. Anyone who aspires to greatness must serve the rest; whoever wants to rank first among you must serve the needs of all." For politics, whether in the Augustan age or in modern democratic society, is the art of imposing one's will upon others. The saying leaves no room for this within the Christian community. If one believes the imposition of one's will is wise and necessary, one must leave the Christian community to do it. This saying is as close as the Gospels come to directions on the Christian administration of political power. I cannot say that such administration is possible; it has certainly never been done, and in the modern world of politics the one who tried it would most certainly be a patsy. The image of political power is the Godfather; he surely got things done.

There is another Gospel passage, not a saying of Jesus and not a memory of a historical event; it is a parable or myth, but it says something about what the attitude of Jesus was thought to be. This is the story of the temptation in which Satan offers Jesus all the kingdoms of the world if he will adore the tempter. Now this is about as clear an offer of political power as one could think of; of course it is unreal and, as I shall try to make clear in another essay, Satan is quite an unreal being. But the reality of which he is a symbol is quite real. The story never questions that political power was Satan's to give, nor that accepting it was to engage in a compact with the devil. This is a harder saying about politicians than I would dare to utter; I am only quoting. But the fictitious answer to this fictitious offer was to tell Satan, in our coloquial language, to get lost. I find the meaning of the temptation narrative quite unambiguous, and it is for those who believe that it says nothing to the drive for political power to explain how they make it meaningless. It may not be an urgent question, or not even a serious question; but it is unfortunate that liberation theologians find discussion beneath them. And to return where I began, as long as this condition persists I cannot support them.

Chapter Ten

POVERTY AND WEALTH

COUNTING of words is a means of somewhat limited value to determine what the author or authors of a piece of writing thought was important. I say of somewhat limited value because I know that some things I think important are rarely in my speech; other things may be much in my speech but for a limited period of time, or only in restricted areas of conversation. With these reservations, and working on memory rather than on a recent count, not easily available at the moment, I believe I am correct in stating that the love of one's neighbor is the topic most frequently mentioned in the Gospels. No one disputes that Jesus thought this was important. Among other topics most frequently mentioned are wealth and poverty. That Jesus thought these were important has been disputed. The preceding chapter arose from recent and current disputes about their importance in Christianity.

In New Testament times poverty and wealth did not mean what they mean in contemporary western Europe and North America. Scott Fitzgerald could have said much more significantly of the first century that the rich were different. Poverty and wealth in the Hellenistic-Roman world were more like poverty and wealth in most of Asia, Africa and apparently all of Central and South America. The wealth was concentrated in the hands of a very few people, and the extreme of poverty reached a point of destitution which is unknown in the United States, and which always shocks visitors from Europe and North America when they experience it elsewhere in the world. Only when they experience it do they understand why we Americans, all of us, are the rich to the rest of the world. The few rich in the Roman world

118

enjoyed all that their world could give them; the poor, who may have been 95% of the population, lived marginally, in the sense that they were not sure on any given day where the next day's food would come from—or often in some regions whether it would come. Death from starvation was not a remote threat for most of the inhabitants of the Roman world.

Jesus was one of the poor, although recently some have pointed out that he was not one of the destitute, in the sense that a village carpenter must have belonged to the middle class. In the New Testament world there was no middle class; a Palestinian village wife did not think her morning wasted if she spent all of it in a successful search for a lost coin of small value. Jesus himself is quoted as saying that he had no place to sleep, which does not translate into middle-class genteel poverty. Our own attitude towards poverty is revealed by our refusal to accept the plain fact that Jesus was dirt poor—to avoid other less elegant expressions. On that social level, as in the war-ravaged economy of Isaiah 3:6-7, the man with a shirt is elected mayor. These were the poor to whom Jesus proclaimed the good news, and whom he called blessed—an unfortunate translation; one catches the spirit of the phrase by some such paraphrase as "You lucky poor," and one wonders whether it was not received with the Galilean equivalent of the Bronx cheer. For centuries Christians have evaded the reality of the poverty of Jesus by taking refuge in Matthew's phrase, "poor in spirit"; the refuge is vain, because poor in spirit means the dispirited, the discouraged, the desperate; it is synonymous with the meek, those who do not resist, and those who are starving for justice, to whom the world denies a square deal. In the world of Jesus as in other worlds the poor were the oppressed. What good news did Jesus have for them? Not the good news that a turn of the wheel of providence would impoverish and subject the oppressors and make them, the poor, rich and powerful oppressors. This might be suggested by a line from the Magnificat (Luke 1:52-53), but it is not a part of the good news proclaimed by Jesus. Nor does the proclamation exhibit the candid hostility toward the rich as a class found in James 5:1-6, although the theme of wealth acquired through oppression is found in both.

Actually the Gospels have little to say to the rich directly; Jesus did not encounter the really wealthy of the Roman world. The only genuinely wealthy person he ever met personally—the meeting is attested only by Luke—was probably Herod Antipas. The words of the Gospels about wealth have the tone of unreality which betrays no personal experience of the world of wealth—something like the celebrated story of the millionaire's daughter who was asked to write a story about a poor family. The whole family, she wrote, was poor—the parents, the children, the butler, the maids, the footmen, the gardeners, the grooms and the chauffeurs. People like Crassus (from whom, I believe, we have the word "crass") and Lucullus, who left his name to a style of dining (preserved in recent years in the name of the most expensive restaurant in Beirut), did not live in backwoods areas like Palestine; they preferred the gracious living of the large cities. Poppaea, Nero's wife, who demanded the milk of 500 she-asses daily for her bath, was regarded by Roman satirists as extravagant. Horace makes fun of a wealthy Roman who fattened the lampreys served as delicacies at his table on the flesh of his slaves. The wit may be based on fiction—I have forgotten; but the point is that if it were based on fact, the owner would have broken no law. The members of the Jerusalem priestly aristocracy and the few village rich men (like Zaccheus) whom Jesus addressed were in the minor leagues of wealth. What Jesus said about wealth supposes that one need not have great wealth, or even any wealth, in order to be greedy. The poor are not excluded from avarice by their state of life.

There was a widespread feeling in the ancient world, not dead in modern times, that great wealth is amassed by dishonesty—that every rich man is a thief or the heir of a thief. I cannot deal with this popular prejudice, and I think we may call it that. I believe the Gospels reflect it, just as they reflect the popular prejudice that the earth is flat, the middle layer of a three-decker universe. Antecedently I classify such general remarks about a class under the same heading with similar general remarks passed about such classes as blacks, Jews, Latin-Americans—and Catholic priests. Jesus came close to excluding the wealthy from the kingdom of God; he is quoted in all three Synoptic Gospels as saying that they will enter the kingdom when a camel passes through a needle's eye (Mark 10:25; Matthew 19:24; Luke 18:25). Efforts to evade the plain meaning of the moral impossibility stated (with some exaggeration, but stated clearly) in this text show how hard it has been for Christians to believe it. Yet Jesus said this with reference to a man who had sought and refused a clear statement on how to get into the kingdom: give away your wealth, stop being wealthy. There is nothing complicated or obscure about these directions. I remember reading many years ago in a source I can no longer trace (and therefore, I suppose, to be read here with critical interest) how many of the great American foundations for education and research were funded with conscience money with which the robber barons who gave the money hoped to assuage their guilt feelings. It certainly beats spending the money on the milk of she-asses for bathing, or yachts.

Jesus is once recorded as speaking severely about mere acquisition (Luke 12:16-21). The man who amasses wealth which he must leave to unknown heirs is called a fool. This epithet expresses extreme moral disapproval in Hebrew and

Aramaic, but the saying does not go beyond folk wisdom,
from which it may well be derived. He also spoke with disapproval of luxurious living, although such remarks as those
which ridicule people who live in palaces and dress in soft
garments (Matthew 11:8) again do not go beyond such folk
wisdom as that expressed by the Greek sage Diogenes. But the
rich man who dressed in fine garments and dined sumptuous-
ly is cursed not just for gracious living but for indifference to
the man who was starving at his door. One's treasure is where
one's heart is—another piece of folk wisdom? And if one's
heart is with one's wealth, it is not with one's neighbor. Jesus
finds fault with possession when it is unaccompanied by
awareness of the needs of others. He speaks as if acquisition
itself demonstrated such unawareness. Jesus did not theorize.
If you do help those in need right around you—and in his
world the wealthy needed to look no farther than their door-
steps—then you have too much, and like the rich man in his
parable, you will die and be buried in hell. I use his figure of
speech, which not everyone may like; perhaps they can tell me
that the figure means that nobody is really going to hold
anything against you.

If Jesus was not speaking directly to the wealthy like
Crassus and Lucullus, what was he saying to those whose
possessions by any standards were only slightly in excess of
the possessions of their neighbors? I have said that the world
of Jesus was a world with no middle class. I am at times impatient with remarks that our world has changed so much that
the sayings of Jesus are no longer applicable. In this context
this seems to mean that because a large number of people are
only moderately wealthy, they are excused from sharing their
modest superfluity with the destitute. We have provided a
government whose benevolence to the needy relieves us of
personal concern. Talk about renouncing wealth to the
Rockefellers, the Vanderbilts and the Kennedys, not to us

who can barely make the payments on the house, two cars, food and utilities, and still hope for a vacation and something put aside for college for the children and for retirement. I am not going to say that this sounds hollow. I do not know that Jesus would change a word if he were addressing the American middle class instead of Palestinian peasants—except that he might be slow to address the modern audience as "You lucky poor."

I do not know how the people of the New Testament times, whether Romans, Greeks or Palestinian Jews, lived without our equivalent of "the system," that nameless non-person who is to blame for everything that we know is wrong but cannot be righted. I suppose for many the demons served the purpose. We have learned to talk about the system the way Paul talked about sin—except Paul said that Jesus has overcome sin. We never say that Jesus has overcome the system— or society, or the economy. We do not believe that he has, and why should we want him to? With its failures the system provides more wealth to more people than any system ever devised; who wants to take the risks involved in changing it? If the system were a god and we gave it a name, the name would be Mammon. Like the real God, his power is beyond searching and his works surpass understanding. Say "It is the system," or "It is society" or "It is the economy"and you have given as complete a theological answer as if you had said, "It is God."

It is almost meaningless to say to oneself or to another, "You are the system"—as meaningless as if one said, "You are God"; but I shall try. I grew up in a soft coal mining area. Since my father was not a miner, we were never the really poor; we would rather have said that we got by, which the really poor did not do. When I read in my mature years the angry shout of John L. Lewis, "There is blood on that coal," I knew vaguely what he meant. That kept none of us from burning coal—even those who were so poor that they had to go down to the freight yards and pick up the spills from the gondola cars. Much later in life I took an auto trip from Los Angeles to Yosemite in July, right through the heart of California's Central Valley. I was then educated enough to feel a sense of guilt at eating any fruit for a while; but the feeling passed. After all, we have to have fruit and vegetables, and the system gives them to us at prices we can afford. They are no longer luxuries for the rich— are we the rich? There was once a saying among Irish-Americans about those who tried so hard to be lace-curtain that they had fresh fruit in the house even when no one was sick.

A further enlightenment came to me later in life when I made a trip to the countries of East Africa. A result of that trip was a taste of guilt in my coffee. The earnings of the coffee pickers—whole families including the aged, women and children—have not been raised since the days of the wicked planters. Like the grape pickers, if they were paid any more, we—the system—would not buy what they picked. Do I need coffee badly enough to pay them more than four (for a child) or eight (for an adult) shillings a day? It is easier to blame the planter, the shipper, the middle man or some multinational cartel and continue to eat fruit and grind coffee beans on which, as John L. Lewis said, there is blood. Anyway why worry about the children? There are no schools for them to attend anyway; bean pickers need no education, and we must have low paid bean pickers if we are to continue to drink coffee.

Delos does not look so bad compared with the system in which we live and which we are. The basic luxury of the wealthy of earlier times was cheap abundant personal service on demand. When you come right down to it, that is still the basic luxury of the wealthy, now extended to the middle class. Perhaps Crassus and Lucullus and Poppaea were as unconscious of the human costs of the gracious comfortable lifestyle as the modern middle class is of what its standard of living costs many others of whom it is unaware. Could Jesus have meant that in his parable of Dives and Lazarus?

A friend, recently arrived from Europe, was being taken on a tour of the local cultural centers such as art galleries. The friend was somewhat surprised when I observed that she was being taken to see collections of robbers' booty. I mentioned no names; if their descendants do not know how the family fortunes were founded, they certainly do not want to be told. About the great European collections of loot amassed by bandits such as those of the Louvre, the Uffizi, the Vatican, the British Museum, the Escorial and others too numerous to mention, reserve is unnecessary; the origins of these collections are too well known. Like the coal of Mr. Lewis, these artistic prizes are smeared with blood. We, who have inherited these collections from the original looters, apparently do not find the blood offensive. I do not know that anyone has ever written a history of art in terms of its human costs; art is a sacred cow in whose name any crime is pardonable. Opening these collections to the public seems to be thought a form of restitution; one wonders whether the public which views them simply becomes a sharer of stolen goods. If we sometimes worry whether we can afford table grapes or coffee in a world which has so many poor, is there not some reason to worry about whether we can afford the Mona Lisa and the Venus di Milo? Several famous American robber barons richly endowed universities where the sons and daughters of the affluent might receive the education befitting the same. This too is regarded as a restitution of plunder. Unfortunately it does not reach those from whom it was stolen.

Perhaps the greatest achievement of modern technology is in communications. But the communications have not brought the men and women of the world any closer in human amity. They have lengthened and strengthened the arm of acquisitiveness. Where Lucullus and Crassus reached over an area less extensive than that of modern Europe, the modern Luculli and Crassi span oceans and dominate continents with an intricate network of trade and bondage. I mentioned a few examples known to me, not being a student of the movements of trade and commerce. The more I learn, the less I want to know about how many people are exploited to furnish me and my kind with what we ridiculously call necessities. Dives in the Gospel of Luke was buried in hell because he did nothing; a man was starving on his doorstep, and he did nothing. Modern communications have laid the starving of the world at my doorstep.

I have expressed myself with probably more feeling than the subject demands or good taste permits. I do so because I think we habitually excuse ourselves from thinking that the words of the Gospel about wealth can possibly refer to us. Let us not be too quick to identify with the beggar Lazarus, or to think that Jesus has said the kingdom of heaven is ours because we are poor. In the first place, we are probably not poor; in the second place, Jesus spoke, as we have seen, to the poor and not to the rich. Somehow or other he never quite said that because you are poor you have got it made with God. It was to the poor that he addressed warnings against cupidity and avarice; these are not vices which only the wealthy can practice. It was to the poor that he recommended sharing what they had with those who have less. It was to the poor that he forbade the use of violence in their own defense—violence which the poor of his world, like the poor of ours, could exercise only against those as poor as themselves. It was to the poor that he recommended bearing injuries and forgiving wrongs; then, as now, the poor had far more opportunity to practice these virtues than the affluent. It was neither Jesus nor Paul but that mysterious somebody known to critics as "Deutero-Paul" (you will pardon the expression) who wrote to the poor of an early Christian community: "If anyone will not work, neither let him eat" (2 Thessalonians 3:9). I am not sure that Jesus or Paul would disclaim this shockingly illiberal sentiment; they might have thought that freeloading was a form of exploitation of the poor.

What would Jesus have said to the moral jungle which often seems to be the ultimate development of modern large cities? I do not know why we should think that he did not address it, or why a social fact which is not new should demand substantial alterations in what we believe is his teaching; I ask readers to notice the reservation. The congestion of the poor in crime-infested slums is at least as old as imperial Rome. The guerrilla warfare between rich and poor may be as old as mankind itself. In this warfare folk heroes like Robin Hood who robbed the rich and gave to the poor loom large. I have never personally investigated Robin Hood to verify or refute my suspicion that, viewed from close up, he might be a non-hero like Jesse James, a bully and killer without conscience, but still venerated as a folk hero in some parts of Missouri. Nevertheless, most of the victims of the jungle warfare are the poor, who are preyed on by their fellow-poor as much as by the rich. I think Jesus addressed this problem; unfortunately, he never suggested that the only sin of the poor was their poverty, or that sharing the wealth, which he certainly recommended, would without further ado produce a community governed by peace and harmony. Jesus had this thing about sin; in modern social thought this is certainly regarded as a large blind spot in his thinking, even worse because he seemed to think that sin was the work of the sinner, not of some nameless impersonal thing called society—or the system, as mentioned earlier. Jesus obviously, as we have seen repeatedly, identified himself with the poor. No one can stretch that identity so far as to identify him with the poor who oppress their fellow-poor. He was crucified with bandits, but that hardly makes him one of them. In Luke's account Jesus approves the bandit who admitted that he got what he deserved.

That community governed by peace and harmony will be created when all of us willingly accept the directions of Jesus on how it is to be brought about. The poor should not think that Jesus imposes burdens only on them. After all, he does demand that the rich abandon their riches in order to enter the kingdom of God. That the rich do not follow these clear instructions does not invalidate his instructions to those whose contributions to a community of peace and harmony cannot be made by the renunciation of their personal wealth. His instructions to them to bear injuries and to forgive those who wrong them rest with equal severity upon the wealthy. Neither the rich nor the poor have done a great job in making this Gospel teaching a reality in the human jungle. If we are to invoke a revolution which will forcibly separate the rich from their riches, shall we also invoke a revolution which will forcibly impose the forgiveness of enemies and the love of one's enemies upon all the members of the human jungle? The thought is absurd; some features of the Gospel are so obviously meaningless unless they are done freely from inner conviction that to think of imposing them by force is to confess that we do not believe they can be done. But a single piece of the Gospel like the redistribution of wealth seems so easy to impose by force that the temptation to replace inner conviction with force seems irresistible. And do we not end up with a human jungle which is still a jungle with different beasts as kings?

I do not claim that Jesus presented an easy program for dealing with wealth and poverty. It just beats any other. It is simple, but it is certainly not easy, nor does it relieve us of thought and suffering. This part of the Gospel was thoroughly grasped by Francis of Assisi. If the whole of Italy had gone after the holy man of Assisi, Italy might never have experienced the Renaissance. Just think of it. But it is an impossible supposition. They would have burned Francis as they burned Savonarola.

Chapter Eleven

LOVING ONE'S NEIGHBOR

THAT well-known contemporary philosopher Charlie Brown once said something like, "I love my neighbor all right; it's people I can't stand." Charlie, as usual, summed up the problem in a nutshell. Love, like hatred, is easily given to abstractions, much less easily to living, breathing persons who are so much like us it sometimes frightens one. Creative writers from Homer to Erich Maria Remarque have told us how the enmity of war dissolves when war is reduced to a naked personal combat between men who really have nothing personal to quarrel about. On the other side, people will be generous to the sick and poor with contributions of money and food, but the same people will be slower to minister personally to the bodily needs of these dirty stinking victims of disease and malnutrition. This is not said by way of criticism; if one cannot at once share the life and the pains of the unfortunate, it is some service to strengthen the hands of those who have stronger stomachs. I merely try to illustrate the point that good will or bad will is shown more easily to people whom we do not see or know.

So when Jesus, quoting Leviticus 19:18, said that one must love one's neighbor as oneself, he did not recommend a love of humanity, which is an abstraction (although Charlie Brown noticed that we have made an abstraction even of the neighbor). The Hebrew word is paralleled in Leviticus 19:17-19 by the word "brother" (a member of your kinship group) and "fellow man" and "fellow countryman" (members of a wider social group, although still limited in the ancient world to people of one's acquaintance). In other contexts the same Hebrew word refers to the person next to one,

130

either by design or by chance; it is also used for objects in the same sense. Thus the neighbor is not merely the adjoining dweller; the neighbor is also the person next to one in a line or in any gathering of people, or with whom one falls into conversation or even meets in a chance encounter on the highway. The "neighbor" is the person next in line at the market, or standing next to one on the bus. The neighbor is, so to speak, the point of one's immediate contact with the human community.

When the author of Leviticus specifies the "love" which one is to show the neighbor, like to the love which one has for oneself, he becomes quite distressingly practical at a low level. Nothing here like the words of Jesus in the Gospel of John: "No one has greater love than to lay down his life for his friends." No, the lawmaker simply avoids the common vices of life in community: do not hate your neighbor, even if you find fault with him (it seems he might have added, if he finds fault with you), and do not cherish a grudge. The author certainly knew where the trouble lies. But he is concerned with the problems of daily human contact, not with rare occasions. His practical recommendations cannot be fulfilled when one leaps over one's neighbor to love the broader world of humanity. Such a love of humanity never leaves you and never reaches its object. The lawmaker demands that you love those who rub against you, those who bump you, those who push you and step on your feet.

The Hebrew word translated "love" means a voluntary attachment to persons; it is somewhat improperly used of attachments to objects or abstractions, much as in English we say "I love money" or "I love my country" (or "I love soft-shelled crabs"), quite well aware that it does not mean the same thing as when one says, "I love my wife." Objects or abstractions cannot reciprocate the sentiment; we think of love as an exchange. Clearly the love of one's neighbor prescribed in Leviticus is mutual; but the individual can only give or withhold his own love, whether it is reciprocated or not. Hatred is forbidden. The explanation of the commandment is illustrated by the saying of St. Ignatius Loyola that love is shown in deeds rather than in words. This will become clearer when we review what Jesus says about the love of one's neighbor.

I have been at some pains to set forth that Leviticus prescribes a love which is immediate and concretely active in order to set the background for the somewhat mischievous paraphrase of the commandment attributed to Jesus in Matthew 5:43. Leviticus does not proscribe hatred of one's enemy —probably the foreigner, the alien, the stranger, not the neighbor as described above. Nor does Jesus accept this interpretation. It very probably described a popular misunderstanding which limited the commandment to members of one's group; and one may remark in passing that if it were observed even within one's social group, that group would be far ahead of mankind in general. Jesus rejects the popular interpretation and keeps the immediate and concretely active character of the love prescribed in the commandment.

In all three synoptic Gospels the saying of Jesus about the love of one's neighbor is given in answer to a question; the three Gospels are at variance, however, on the exact quotation of the discussion (Mark 12:28-34; Matthew 22:34-40; Luke 10:25-37). In all three Gospels Jesus places the love of one's neighbor on the same level of obligation as the love of God. The original dialogue seems to have been put in the terms of rabbinic discourse. The rabbis counted 613 different commandments in the five books of Moses (the Law or the Torah). These were further subdivided into 365 positive commandments and 248 prohibitions. To bring some order into such a large number of frequently conflicting obligations, the rabbis graded the commandments according to weight; in a conflict of duties the "heavier" commandments always outweighed the "lighter." Jesus makes the two commandments of love equal in weight and absolutely the heaviest; it is not conceived that there could be a conflict between the love of God and the love of one's neighbor. Matthew's phrase, "From these two hang the whole Law and the Prophets [that is, the entire Scriptures]," seems to allude to the weight of the commandments; the "lighter" hangs from the heavier." Paul, trained in rabbinical discourse, understood Jesus quite well when he wrote twice (Romans 13:9; Galatians 5:14) that he who keeps the commandment to love one's neighbor has kept all the other commandments (611 of them). Some will say that this oversimplifies Christian morality in the modern world; but I am just quoting. We shall return to this point.

So distinctive in character is the love that is mandated that the New Testament writers do not easily find a word for it. The Greek words, like our English word *love,* are becoming meaningless. When we have no word to express the deepest personal attachment except the same word which we use to describe our craving for ice cream or our joy in dancing, one feels a certain poverty of language. And therefore the deepest love is shown not by saying something but by doing something, as St. Ignatius Loyola said. As we have seen and shall see further, this is true also of the love of the neighbor. The Greek words which we translate *love* are three: the first is *philia,* which designates the love of friends, and the second is *eros,* which designates sexual love. The first of these might do for the love of one's neighbor, except that *philia* suggests feelings of affection which may not be present in the love of one's neighbor. Hence the New Testament employs the third word, rather late and rare in classical Greek, to signify an attitude for which classical Greek had no word; the word is *agape* and its corresponding verb, *agapan.* The desire to find a distinctive word for a distinctive sentiment is reflected in

Latin also; the earliest Latin translators used the quite late and rare word *caritas* for Christian love of the neighbor, which passed into English as *charity*.

That this word designates a quite distinctive sentiment is illustrated by something which I heard said many years ago: "I will be charitable to him, but I don't like him." The remark certainly showed a very common misunderstanding of the distinctive character of the love of one's neighbor, as well as a failure to grasp the prohibition of hatred in Leviticus. I have shared this misunderstanding often enough over a long life to quote the remark with no feeling of superiority. Were the nature of "charity" truly grasped, both by those who confer it and by those who receive it, it would not have become a proverbial retort of the poor and the needy to say, not without bitterness, "I do not want your charity." No one could want anything more. We shall return to this.

Luke reports that Jesus answered the question who is the neighbor by telling the parable of the good Samaritan (Luke 10:29-37). The parable is found only in Luke; but it is so much at home in Palestinian Judaism that no one thinks the Gentile Luke is its author. The choice of the Samaritan as the most unlikely neighbor deserves some attention. Jesus did not mention a Roman, certainly a representative of a hated foreign oppressive power, nor a "Greek," the word used generally for neighboring peoples, despised by the Jews because of their religion (or lack of it) and their immorality. Instead Jesus picks a Samaritan, a neighbor in the sense of geographical proximity, again despised because of his religion, which was not paganism but basically the same religion as that of the Jews but without the orthodoxy of Pharisaism, and a member of a community with whom Jews had an ethnic kinship which they preferred not to recognize. The Samaritan was indeed a neighbor in the sense that he was near; the Jew might easily encounter a Samaritan, but he might rarely encounter a Roman or a Greek. As when he pointed out the poor, Jesus, asked who is a neighbor, said, "Look around you, or behind you, and see the first person you dislike or hate; that is your neighbor." The Jew hated the Samaritan not because of anything personal, but because he belonged to the wrong group. If Jesus were telling the parable now where he told it then, he would replace the Samaritan with a Palestinian Arab. Were he to tell it in southern California where I now live, he would make it equally concrete in another way—and he might change the parable as often as he changed his audience.

The parable answers the question who is the neighbor so sharply and so vividly that few critics would question my personal belief that Luke has preserved an authentic saying of Jesus; they would wonder, as I do, how the saying escaped Matthew and Mark. They might suspect, as I do, that Jewish writers felt a sting in the parable which Luke, who probably would not have known a Samaritan from a Zulu, would not have recognized. Matthew makes the same point in more general (and less vivid) terms when he defines the love of one's neighbor as the love of one's enemies (Matthew 5:43), and adds that there is nothing remarkable in mutual love and affection; this is exhibited by those whom Jews put at the bottom of the moral ladder.

We homilists have long been missing the point, perhaps, in the parable of the good Samaritan—or at least part of the point. We have proposed the Samaritan as an example of one who helps even a hostile stranger, but we forget that Jesus was speaking to Jews. The Jew in the story is proposed as an example of one who receives help from one whom he believes to be a hostile stranger. They only way he can show himself a neighbor is to accept gracefully and gratefully the assistance rendered by one who has shown himself a neighbor, even though he would rather die than accept help from a Samaritan. Would he really? I said earlier that I would return to the point that charity is often seen as something odious, patronizing, an affront to one's personal dignity. If the love of one's neighbor is shown by help in need, love would seem to demand that those helped be not resentful, that they do not accept the assistance as a right. To accept help is indeed an attack on one's personal dignity; perhaps the traveler in the parable thought so. But the Samaritan attacked his personal dignity much less than the robbers who had stripped him and left him half-dead. It is extremely difficult to render assistance without patronizing, and extremely difficult to accept it without hating your benefactor. But if the assistance cannot be done well, then it should be done badly. Personal dignity is a price which must be paid by anyone who tries to observe the commandment of love.

Matthew's saying, as quoted above, makes it clear that love of neighbor which does include the love of one's enemy does not extend beyond the minimum. The question of who is one's neighbor Jesus has answered; we must answer for ourselves the question of who is our enemy. This question is large enough to deserve treatment in a separate essay. For the present I may say that very few of us have personal enmities that are mortal; those few who do have them have personal problems which cannot be resolved by reading a short essay. Our mortal enmities are imposed upon us by the social groups of which we are members; our mortal enmities, meaning enmities which can issue in killing, lie between us and people whom we do not even know personally. Because this topic will be treated later more extensively, let me say, again for the present, that the disciple to whom Jesus spoke can simply have no enemies, personal or social. The disciple may be hated—in fact Jesus probably promised his disciples that they would be hated if they lived this way—but the disciple does not hate. The person does not exist with whom the disciple finds reconciliation impossible. But the fact is that if we do not share the hatreds of our social group (our "neighbors") the group may turn on us and rend us.

Jesus, as I have said earlier, was extremely realistic and extremely practical, in spite of some widespread misconceptions about his relations to "the real world" and "real life." In Matthew 25:31-46 there is an imaginary scene often incorrectly called a last judgment scene. I suppose many travelers to the Near East, like me, remember the shocked surprise with which they saw, a day or two after their arrival, herdsmen separating sheep from goats in the common pasture, and recognized this living reenactment of the saying of Jesus. The parable (we may call it that) seems to make the entire judgment of personal worth, of human success or failure, depend on how one has responded to human need. The love of one's neighbor is not sentiment nor an abstraction. The question is not how you feel about your neighbor but what have you done for him; I know I oversimplify, but I think I may blame Matthew. It is, as I said, very realistic and very practical; it is also terribly personal and terribly immediate. It is understood that the parable does not take account of those who might answer, "We voted for public welfare," or, "We gave to the United Way." I do not say that the parable would continue, "You are goats; you did not want to get personally involved." But anyone who wishes to share my apprehension is free to do so. During the American Civil War it was possible for a man of means to hire a substitute if he were drafted for military service. It has struck me that we who contribute through taxes and welfare agencies are like the wealthy who hired substitutes to do the dirty work while we keep our hands clean. Well, I suppose it beats doing nothing, but by how much? We gave some of our goods, but did we give ourselves?

Yet what are these services which are judged so essential

for achieving success as a person? They are not great; those who do them are not remembered as heroes and heroines by a grateful nation. (Mark Twain, not an outstanding religious person, once wrote that those who are called heroes sometimes work just the opposite of what Jesus in this passage makes the test; as a result of their heroism people are killed, they starve, are impoverished, driven from their homes.) The services called for can be very small, meeting no more than a passing need and, as many say, leaving the problems unsolved. Jesus, to repeat what I fear I used previously, did not say, I was hungry and you formed a study group or had a demonstration against hunger. To some degree they are services within the reach of everyone who is not actually hungry, thirsty, naked, homeless, ill or imprisoned. The world is divided into those who need help and those who can help, with more or with less. Each one knows to which group he or she belongs. It takes no wealth, no special talent, no special skill to help another with what one has. The widow was praised for dropping a small coin in the poor box; the same praise would not have been rendered Dives for the same contribution, while he mumbled that times are hard and you have to think of the future.

I have spoken of the reciprocal element in this community of neighbors already: the readiness of those in need to swallow their pride and accept help even when it is clumsily given. No one is self-sufficient, and those who think they are will learn with a shock that they are not. Self-sufficiency is not a native talent; it cannot be earned and it cannot be purchased. Everyone must sooner or later accept his dependent position in the human community, humiliating as it may be. When I read that someone has died alone of illness or starvation or frostbite, I know they went to great pains for what may have been their successful effort to go it alone. But it says much about the decline of neighborliness in modern industrial society that these deaths can happen in congested "neighborhoods" (what a gross abuse of the word) full of uncaring people. These deaths do not occur in primitive African villages. Where were the welfare agencies? They are not instituted to care, but to do the dirty work for the uncaring.

I said above that Paul reduced all of the Law—which means all moral obligation—to the one obligation of love of the neighbor. Robert Browning, again not an outstanding religious person, put this in a short poem which modern readers find corny. I said that Paul seemed to interpret the mind of Jesus correctly, as far as we can judge from his collected sayings. The modern Christian in a complex industrialized civilization says, or is tempted to say, that this is a vast oversimplification. Love, we are told, is a simple solution which does not solve the complex problems we have. I have never heard a clear statement of how many problems hatred solves. In a world dominated by experts we trust the experts to analyze problems and propose solutions; we are not going to listen to anyone who says that our problems will be solved by something so simple that a child can grasp it. Whether we admit it or not, this is to say that Jesus no longer has anything meaningful to say to the modern industrialized world. It has accurately been called a post-Christian world, and our experts are teaching us how to live, or rather how to survive, in a world in which Jesus has died not to rise.

But, thank God, he is irrepressible. His words about the love of the neighbor were addressed to the little people, who are not faced with the solution of world of international problems of politics, diplomacy, war and finance, and cannot wait for the great minds to solve these problems before they can live at peace with their neighbors. If the little people paid less attention to the great minds which create more problems than they solve, perhaps the great minds would find themselves out of business. The experts have devised complicated rules of conduct which tell little people how to evade the love of their neighbor, or at least the love of some of their neighbors, or how it is their duty to their nation, their class, or their church not to love some of their neighbors—or in any case to make no loving movement unless their neighbor makes a movement first. One who follows these rules faithfully may with a good conscience behave like a bastard to his neighbor; and that is the best way to survive in a post-Christian world.

If the complications of Christian living in the modern world are so great that we cannot solve the daily problems of human relations without recourse to a corps of experts, have we not returned to the yoke of the Law with its 613 commandments interpreted by a corps of experts? Certainly to resolve one's doubts by following the course dictated by love will not secure one against all mistakes. If the corps of experts could promise this, they would have more to recommend them. There is enough room for expert opinion to operate in resolving the conflicting demands which are made upon one's love and in distinguishing genuine from spurious love. Authentic Christians find this less of a problem than those who are less fully committed. The mistakes they make are the mistakes of love, not of not caring or of cruelty. It costs them more, but it costs their neighbors less. Maybe that is the name of the game. Those who love indiscreetly will not be classified with the goats. To love one's neighbor as oneself is not difficult to understand; it is just difficult to do. However one feels about oneself, whatever degree of self-contempt or self-hatred one may reach, however keenly one may be hurt by the sense of one's inadequacy and failure, one can never wish evil for oneself.

Chapter Twelve

FAITH

IN the baptismal rite long in use in the Roman Catholic Church, the minister of baptism greeted the candidate for baptism with the question, "What dost thou ask of the Church of God?" The candidate answered (in person or through the sponsors), "Faith." The minister then asked, "And what does faith bring thee?" to which the candidate answered, "Life everlasting." The ritual, while it is certainly ancient, might have puzzled St. Paul. He would say, I think, "But the church does not give the candidate faith; the candidate must bring faith in order to receive baptism. Faith means that one accepts the good news that God has wrought salvation in Jesus Christ; when one has believed, one must repent of one's sins and through baptism begin a new life in Christ." This answer is derived from what Paul wrote about baptism; and if it is correctly derived, it suggests that the understanding of faith changed somewhat between the New Testament and the development of the ritual of baptism.

And indeed there has been change, changes which came to a head in the Protestant-Catholic quarrels over the meaning of faith which were some of the main issues of division in the Reformation. It is probably safe now to say what is true (in theology it has not always been safe) and observe that the Catholic-Protestant disputes hardened both parties in positions which were one-sided, both of which failed to grasp what faith meant in the Gospels and Epistles. Both Catholic and Protestant theologians now recognize this, and ecumenical conversations in recent years have shown that each can learn from the other. It is tempting to pass a cheap witticism that the whole thing was a ghastly misunderstanding; ghastly

it was, but it was more than a misunderstanding. Certainly
reconciliation demands an agreement based on a common
understanding of biblical faith. It may serve the purpose of
this series to review, however briefly and superficially, what
that understanding may be.

To start from where we are, it is perhaps best to go over
very briefly the Catholic and Evangelical positions on faith;
that is, let us review what most Catholics and most Protestants think they mean when they say, "I believe in God" or
"I believe in Jesus Christ." Catholics mean that they think
that some things God has said are true, that they learn what
these things are from the church, and that they accept these
things as true only on God's authority. Since they learn these
things from the church, the authority of God becomes indistinguishable from the authority of the church; thus
Catholics speak of their "Catholic faith" in a way in which
Protestants never speak of their "Protestant faith."

To Protestants security against error is less important; I
know I oversimplify both positions, but I am trying to state
the popular understanding of communicants of Catholic and
Protestant churches, and no one doubts that popular understanding is oversimplified. Evangelical faith in God and Jesus
Christ is confidence that God and Jesus Christ have done
what they promised; it is trust in their power and good will,
both directed toward us. In precisely that form of faith which
is called evangelical, it means assurance that God has forgiven sins, and I mean the sins of the individual believer. Sins
are forgiven when one believes that they are forgiven; in that
sense evangelical faith saves.

Brief this summary is, and I admit inadequate; and I am
ready to be told about what I left out. I know I left it out; I
am saying that the popular understanding of both Catholics
and Protestants leaves it out too, and often leaves out something very important. Belief in neither view means what it

often means in popular speech: "I think so (but I am not sure)." Or does this popular speech affect the quality of religious belief, whether Catholic or Protestant? Evangelical faith certainly approaches that type of faith expressed when parents and children, or spouses, say to each other, "I believe in you." The Catholic understanding of faith in no way resembles this; it rather resembles the popular meaning of "I believe you" meaning "I believe what you say." Our discussion here turns around the question whether either understanding is faithful to the New Testament idea of faith, meaning mostly the Gospels and Paul. Perhaps I can best show my impartiality by saying that to present New Testament faith as an assurance that personal sins are forgiven is no less a gross misunderstanding than to present it as an assurance that what God has revealed through the Catholic Church is true.

What did Jesus mean, or what did those who reported his words think he meant, when he is alleged to have addressed his disciples on several occasions as "you of little faith?" We can remove from discussion any suggestion that the phrase refers to their failure to accept all of the articles of a creed of faith; Jesus obviously did not mean that. Among other things, the Gospels never report him as proposing a creed of articles of faith. But likewise in almost all contexts the epithet obviously does not refer to failure to believe that God has forgiven personal sins. Most frequently faith is demanded as a condition for a healing; this means that one accepts Jesus as possessing power to heal. It is also a condition for achieving wonders which exceed ordinary strength, or even human power altogether. A demonstration of the power of Jesus to heal is a proof that he has the power to forgive sins. The visible superhuman achievement shows that the invisible achievement lies within the same power. When the disciples are terrified during a storm at sea, they are rebuked for little faith; one who is not terrified, we would say, simply has not grasped the situation. Perhaps it is better for the moment during this discussion not to be stalled on the historical character of this particular episode. We simply notice that one who is not sure that Jesus can deliver from the threatening position of an open boat in a stormy sea is said to lack sufficient faith. When Peter is rebuked for little faith when he fails to walk upon the sea, we are in an almost certainly imaginary episode; and we should no doubt attend to the symbolism of the narrative.

Both the disciples in the boat and Peter walking on the water are charged with little faith because they doubt the ability and will of Jesus to save them—but from what? Jesus elsewhere told his disciples that he who tries to save his life will lose it, and he who is willing to lose his life will find it. Death is not the worst threat which a disciple will meet; and it takes profound faith to believe this. Faith is the assurance that even if one loses one's life one will save it. To put it another way, the disciple must believe that following Jesus and the Gospel are worth not only the risk of one's life, but the certainty of losing it. The peril from which Jesus saves the disciples is the peril of their own weakness and fear, the mortal fear which will tempt them to say that following Jesus and the Gospel is worth a great deal, but not worth one's life. The legends of the early martyrs are full of stories of the vain efforts of the persecutors to kill the martyr, frustrated by miraculous intervention, while the martyr laughed at their efforts to overcome God; but the stories all end with what was a fact for all martyrs, death at the hands of those who finally overcame God. But did they really? What is more marvelous, the quite fictitious stories of such temporary deliverances or the fact of the successful perseverance of the martyrs without such temporary deliverances? The third-century Church Father Tertullian lived before such legends arose when he wrote, "The blood of martyrs is the seed of Christians."

More credible—although devout imagination has been at work here too—is the story of unbelievers who were so impressed by the constant loyalty of Christian believers that they became instant believers. This, and not the legendary futile miracles of temporary deliverances, was their witness to faith; and "martyr" means witness.

Similarly, faith as expressed in the cults of faith healing has always impressed most Christians as an extremely narrow sectarian understanding of faith. Even more narrow was the strange cult of snake handling which was prohibited, I believe, by civil law about a generation or two ago—not very effectively, I think; "little faith" failed to overcome the vicious and venomous instincts of a few diamond-backed rattlesnakes. Yet the cult was based on Mark 16:18, supported by Acts 28:3-6. One must say that the members of this cult stopped reading the New Testament texts on faith with these verses; one may say cautiously something similar about the mainline Protestant and Catholic interpretations mentioned earlier. There is no doubt that several healing stories represent Jesus as demanding faith for a healing, or praising it because it is there already. Yet the fact remains that the sayings of Jesus as a whole, as well as the understanding of the primitive Church, do not leave the impression that this was to be the normal Christian way of dealing with human illness and pain. If it should be, we have left the message of Jesus so far behind us that we might as well give up and start over again; and some might not think that a bad idea anyway.

If faith healing is not the normal way of dealing with human pain and illness, the ministry of compassionate service to the ill, especially to the poor, certainly is. In the time of Jesus, and during the whole Roman period, there was no organized form of assistance for the sick poor. This form of ministry is a Christian invention. The earliest hospitals were what are now called warehouses of the dying; with primitive medicine what else could they be? In the lives of the saints of medieval and early modern times there is almost a refrain of he or she "served the plague-stricken" or he or she "died serving the plague-stricken." Travelers who have stumbled over corpses in the streets of large oriental cities know that hospitals which provided only a more comfortable place to die than the streets and alleys were not a total waste of effort. This ministry took and still takes profound faith; nothing else seems to convey the conviction that it is worthwhile and rewarding. Dedication to this service, like martyrdom, is an impressive witness of faith, far more persuasive than argument. I am not sure that the rather newly developed "health industry," as it is called, is a legitimate successor to this ministry; at least Jesus the healer did not refuse to make house calls. But that is another topic.

The faith which heals also has a symbolic value. Popular belief, lacking even the elementary medical knowledge possessed by Greek scientists, attributed almost all human ills which had no obviously perceptible cause to the malignant activity of demons. As I shall attempt to show in another essay, we cannot share faith which implies this belief. Yet we shall at the same time see that it is a modern delusion to think that because the reality of the demonic world has been proved non-existent the reality of evil has also been proved non-existent. It is very real and very much with us, however it may be conceived; and with the Gospels we are invited to faith in Jesus as the only effective defense against the power of evil, whatever we may call it. The modern sophisticated man and woman may wonder—or indeed may not wonder—whether the power of evil is still aptly called human sin, whether modern learning has finally overcome sin by declaring it non-existent, as our predecessors overcame demonic power by declaring it non-existent. It is probably safe to say that there is something seriously wrong with the human condition;

possibly whether one refuses to call it sin may be less important. It is important whether one admits that faith in Jesus is faith in the only power which is able to diagnose and correct what is wrong. And I think that a faith which moves mountains may be barely enough for this task. Man has literally moved mountains—small ones, it is true, but in finding fulfillment of a biblical text why quibble about size? The mountain of human wickedness—I call it that—still sits there unmoved because faith the size of a mustard seed is missing.

From the consideration of faith as a mover of mountains, together with faith as a source of healing or as a condition of healing, it emerges that faith in the Gospels is presented as a power or as something which connects one with a power. This power enables one to accomplish things which lie beyond the limits of human achievement; it is the power of God. One may grant indeed that the presentation of this power is not without an element of exaggeration found not only in oratory and poetry but also in the popular speech of the Gospels. Such exaggeration should be understood as a component of human discourse which even children grasp—but not wooden literal interpreters of the Bible or of other writings. There is legend of a fourth or fifth century saint named Gregory, called Thaumaturgus (wonder worker), who by prayer once moved a mountain, not to mention other wonders which I have no time to look up. It seemed to early Christians that there should not be a word of Jesus which was left unfulfilled; it was the same type of faith observed in the cult of snake handling (which is less strong on other wonders such as tending the sick poor and reconciliation with one's enemies). The proclamation of the Gospel throughout the Roman world in the less than three centuries between Paul and Constantine by a group of uneducated members of the socially depressed classes without any of the propaganda resources of the ancient world—which would have included art and written and spoken language—was not without some element of wonder. It was certainly an enduring monument to the faith which moved mountains, if I may be permitted the same exaggeration as Jesus; but what would moving mountains have done for the proclamation of the Gospel? It would have been as effective as the temptation offered to Jesus of a leap headlong from the pinnacle of the temple. The wonders of faith are not promised for vain display or self-aggrandizement. The faith which moves mountains must move through slow and exhausting tasks fulfilled with patient fidelity; it is not as much fun as spectacular stunts which are done quickly, but that seems to be the quite dull and unexciting way in which Jesus accomplished whatever it was he accomplished during his life.

Although the letters of Paul are earlier than the Gospels, it seems that the Gospel understanding of faith is presupposed when Paul makes faith, repentance and baptism the conditions by which one becomes incorporated into Christ. Faith means that one accepts fully and without reservation that Jesus is what he claims to be: that he responds to all human needs, answers all human questions, gives human life meaning and fulfillment. Paul accepted a statement attributed to Peter in Acts, that there is no other name under heaven by which we are saved. Faith meant that one was united to Christ: one died with him and rose with him, and one lived with him, through him and in him. To borrow a phrase which I have borrowed before, Paul did not believe that Jesus was the most important thing; he believed that Jesus was the only thing. Thinking anything less is not faith. Nor does Paul suppose that can be surely and finally achieved at one bold stroke —like moving a mountain. Faith is subject to growth, but also to weakening; it is an attachment to Jesus which is maintained only by unfailing effort of will. I should add that for Paul such single-minded faith in Jesus as Lord and Savior gave security which was proof against any threat. I said above that the disciples had to learn that death is not the worst threat. They had to learn also that faith in Jesus was security against a worse threat, the threat posed by their own malice.

It does appear that New Testament faith in God and Jesus Christ is a quite singular attitude which defies explanation; it seems that such faith is not given to anyone else. How can we define it, or even recognize it? I have suggested, neither subtly nor humbly, that two of the major credal traditions in western Christianity have not succeeded in capturing it; this is not so rash as it seems. I have simply accepted some of the criticism uttered by each side. Perhaps the problem lies not so much in the sentiment itself as in the object of the sentiment. Our responses to God must be human, but we feel that they should be different from our responses to other persons. The difference, however, we do not know how to define.

· We are all familiar with the faith that we and others have in ourselves. And I think I may distinguish true faith from mere confidence, the assurance of "I know I can do it" from the sometimes brash and unfounded confidence of "I think I can do it." I once was taxed by a fellow student with arrogance because I said—in answer to a question—that I had studied enough for an examination. He did not understand that I had a long history of successful examinations, that I knew as well as anyone else in my age group how to study, that experience assured me that I had studied more than enough to prepare for an oral examination. My mistake was in showing my faith in myself instead of saying politely that I, like him, would be cramming up to the last minute before the exam. He did not have faith in himself. Such faith is shown by experienced artists before a performance and by very successful athletes before competition. To those who lack their endowments and the preparation they make for such events it looks much like arrogance. They may lose the competition, but it is unthinkable that they should not do well. Perhaps it does take arrogance to think that their doing well will beat anyone else who does well. The experienced speaker or writer may have a bad day, and perhaps only he and a few close friends will know that he has laid an egg; but his faith in his proved ability will not allow him to fear that he will be at a loss for words or for ideas. I have no doubt that a similar faith in their own powers animates a fire company when they confront a blaze which looks to less experienced eyes as if it were going to be a reenactment of the Chicago fire. But this leads us to another and more closely relevant aspect of human faith, the faith of the members of a group in each other.

One of the most exciting sights of team sports is the cooperation of the members of a team who anticipate each other's moves. In football, basketball and baseball it is impressive to see the ball thrown apparently without looking and at random to an empty spot and to see another member of the team apparently materialize out of the ground or the floor to receive what is thrown. The sight of aerial acrobats who take off from a swinging trapeze at the one moment when the catch is possible looks foolhardy; as a matter of fact it appears to be less dangerous than driving a car. If drivers took the time and trouble to train and discipline themselves which aerialists take, we might have as much faith in our fellow motorists as aerialists have in each other. Members of teams have faith in each other, meaning that they trust each other to be where they are supposed to be when they are supposed to be and that they can do what they are supposed to do. It is not blind faith; it is based on disciplined training, practice and shared experience. It is also limited to the area of competition; there is a baseball legend that Tinker and Evers (perhaps unduly famous) never spoke to each other. To make double plays they did not have to.

We have long been told that our faith in God and in Jesus

Christ should be like the faith of a child in its parents. I fear that adults cannot seriously recreate that sentiment. But we are no strangers to faith; we depend on it daily. A scholar who will say that a trained critical mind makes faith impossible would, if he meant this, spend most of his life checking the footnotes of other scholars. We adults have learned that faith in oneself or faith in a team does not extend to the simple business of being a decent human being. There we all recognize that either alone or with our fellows we cannot hack it. We need help. Five thousand years of civilization have brought us to the point of progress where we are able and seem willing to wipe out humanity to impose our will on others. It is not perhaps altogether fanciful to think of this challenge of faith in God and Jesus Christ as demanding faith like the faith of the aerialist as he or she takes off from the trapeze. Or will it be like a leap from the pinnacle of the temple, of which Jesus said: "Thou shalt not tempt the Lord thy God"?

Chapter Thirteen

THE INSTITUTIONAL CHURCH

NOT only in modern journalism, but even in much theological literature the term "institutional church" has since the early 60s come to have an unpleasant connotation. I do not think I read more into modern writers than they mean when I say that the institutional church implies an opposition to the real or the genuine church, or the church as the body of Christ, or the church as the temple of the Holy Spirit, or the church as the community of love; others may add to this list according to taste. It is implied that the institutional church is all that the church should not be and nothing of what the church should be, or what the church really is. Perhaps some reflections on the reality of the institutional church and on its potential will suit our purpose in this book.

Questions and doubts about the institutional church are at least as old as the heretic Montanus of the second century, who believed that the church needed a new leadership of inspired prophecy. There has been a constant stream of variant belief and practice, in which dissatisfaction with official leadership has ranged from mild criticism to open rebellion. Critics of the institutional church, using the word critic somewhat loosely, have included people as different from each other as Catherine of Siena, Abbot Joachim, Girolamo Savonarola and the Reformers. It would be a long list if I attempted to make it comprehensive. And it is impossible to say that all the critics were heretics and that all the criticisms were lies—even if one might think that identifying the Church of Rome with the Scarlet Woman of Revelations 17, as some Reformers did, was a bit much. On the other hand, when one studies the

Church of the Renaissance, one understands what they had in mind.

Contemporary criticisms of the institutional church seem comparatively mild, and probably less sharp than they might be. There are, and probably always have been, several guilt factors which inhibit criticism of the institutional church, most of which can be summed up in the proverb: "It's an ill bird that fouls its own nest." There is the sentiment felt by most Catholics expressed in the celebrated toast of Commodore Stephen Decatur: "My country, right or wrong! May she always be right; but right or wrong, my country." I regret that I cannot give due credit to the wit who many years ago paraphrased the Commodore's toast thus: "My mother, drunk or sober! May she always be sober; but drunk or sober, my mother." There is the ancient title of Holy Mother given to the church, which suggests that criticism of the institutional church is unfilial blasphemy. Perhaps there is room here for some reflections—shallow perhaps, but better than none—on just what is the institutional church, and how much of the "institution" can be legitimately ascribed to Jesus Christ. The second question I can no more than touch; but no Catholic should be unaware that few if any features of the concrete existing institutional church would be attributed to the direct wishes of Jesus Christ by even the most conservative Roman Catholic theologian. They should know that "faith," which I discussed in a preceding essay, by no biblical warrant can be taken to mean that uncritical, unthinking, total loyalty which is demanded by no one except the leaders of political parties.

In a way which is its own, I know, the institutional church is the "real" church, and I shall try to explain how I believe it does not exhaust the total reality of the church. But the institutional church is the church which is experienced in history; it is the church in which or with which we live and with which we must always deal; it is inescapable. It is hierarchical, it is organized; it is even bureaucratic; it is a false oversimplification to say that bureaucracy or officialdom is not the real church. Neither officialdom nor Dorothy Day incorporates the total reality of the church, although one aspect of the reality may be more attractive than the other. That Jesus perspired is as much a reality as that he spoke the word of the Gospel; but I have never heard of a devotion to the Sacred Sweat. When we accept the whole church, we are no more free to pick and choose what we like than we are when we accept the whole Christ.

But accepting the whole church does not mean a blind and uncritical loyalty of the kind mentioned above. We often close our eyes to certain features of the Incarnate Word which are repugnant to our culture, and by so doing we run the peril of Docetism, the earliest of all heresies, which said that Jesus was not quite real; in a sense, he was too good to be true. There is a kind of Docetism of the church, which echoes the words of Ephesians 5:25-27. "(Christ) gave himself for (the church) to make her holy, purifying her in the bath of water by the power of the word, to present to himself a glorious church, holy and immaculate, without stain or wrinkle or anything of that sort." No interpreter doubts that the author spoke of the eschatological church, what is called the church triumphant, and not of the existing historical church of experience. Such a view of the church is like the Christ triumphant of Byzantine art, never seen or experienced by human eye. The historic church, like the historic Cromwell, has warts. Unlike the great Oliver, it sometimes wishes to be painted without them.

Is it filial loyalty to point out the warts on one's mother? Here one must point out that the appellation of Holy Mother Church (like the appellation of Vicar of Christ) is totally unbiblical. In much of the church from ancient times to the present the members have not experienced a mother; they have experienced that the man in charge was a thief. Little is told us about Judas Iscariot, but three things are sure: (1) he was one of the Twelve; (2) he sold Jesus for money; (3) he killed himself. My mother, honest or thief; may she always be honest; but honest or thief, my mother. I may say that loyalty to Judas would have demanded forgiveness, if he had stayed around to ask for it; but I do not think it would have demanded that I give him a standing ovation as a great shepherd. Are these warts on the mystical body, or are they gangrenous members?

Let us, then, take it for granted that nothing in the past history of the church nor in its present reality raises it above criticism. Are we to assume, on the principle of the bird and its own nest, that the members are not to find fault? If so, it must be because the organized institutional church is equipped with a perpetual self-correcting mechanism—a kind of spiritual gyroscope?—which makes criticism from outside the organization not only unnecessary, but embarrassing and harmful; and I mean the inner organization, what is sometimes called the ruling class; I mean the only possible seat for such a self-correcting device, the hierarchy. Since the hierarchy has included successors of Judas as well as of Peter and John, I do not believe that anyone would seriously urge this; but unless the hostility of the institutional church to criticism arises from something else than a very human resentment at fault-finding, it must arise from some such concealed theological belief. There is no quarreling with the established fact that historically the institutional church has exhibited almost no capacity for self-correction. Bishops have not shown even the capacity to catch the thieves among their brother bishops. I said in an earlier essay that one does not need a complete analysis of the contemporary church to know that one does not live in the Renaissance. Nor does one need a complete analysis to know that the institutional church could use some self-examination (or an audit) about its observance of the Seventh Commandment (the Roman Catholic count).

I do not mean to center this essay upon the administration of the temporal affairs of the church; this business is an illustration of the central thrust of this essay, which is that the institutional church is open to legitimate criticism. It happens to me too; one thing I share with the institutional church is that I almost never receive any criticism I think is legitimate. I have to hope that the illegitimate criticisms do not stumble on the truth. I have no means available to me to silence my critics, or even to conceal the evidence on which they base their criticism.

It is an obvious and inescapable fact that there will be errors in judgment and malicious motives in criticism; one may expect to be rid of these when the institutional church fails to furnish grounds for criticism—that is, when the church becomes the eschatological church, the heavenly Jerusalem descending from heaven like a bride to meet her spouse (Revelations 21). Until the arrival of that great day, we shall have to bear unjust and unkind criticism as we shall have to bear the occasional unkindness, injustice and dishonesty of the institutional church. We should not forget that the institutional church also gives us organized ministry and teaching and organized works of charity. It is precisely her tremendous potential which makes us indignant that that potential is raped for personal gain by little men who turn the church, or their dioceses, or their departments into a vast cookie jar. Perhaps the immortal words of Leo X (undeservedly overshadowed by his predecessor by a few years, Alexander VI) should have been emblazoned as prominently as the words of Jesus, "Thou art Peter": "God has given us the Papacy, let us enjoy it."

There is better biblical warrant for criticism of the institutional church than there is for the patient and grateful silence which is recommended; the image of the faithful should not be the sheep or the lambs, but Balaam's ass, and even the ass finally became critical of its rider. Matthew 18 contains a passage on fraternal correction; it has no parallel in the other Gospels (like Matthew 16:18-19 about the primacy of Peter), but in this context we will not let that disturb us. Like the rest of the Gospels, the passage does not distinguish between those of greater or lesser or no rank in the church (on which I will enlarge below); there is no reason here or elsewhere to exclude the leaders of the church from those who are corrected by their brothers (or sisters), just as there is no reason for excluding the leaders of the church from the scope of fraternal charity. The whole point of the Gospels is that the leaders are just some other guys named Joe; I am reminded of this because I heard an anecdote of a priest who was jawed by an excellent prelate because he spoke of an eminent prelate, then recently created, in terms which betrayed not only friendship and esteem, but undue familiarity. Many years ago I heard of another excellent prelate, now deceased, greeted with the same undue familiarity by an old friend—or so the friend thought—from school days, who responded coldly, "Your Excellency, if you please." If Jesus had only updated his teaching, he would have said, "Call no man Excellency," and certainly not small-bore guns like these two. But Eminence, Excellency, Holiness are symbolic fences or umbrellas against critics. It is quite impossible to think of the fraternal correction of Matthew 18 practiced with men with whom one must first obtain an audience and then greet as Your Excellency. Fraternal correction, no matter how well founded or how gracefully put, is always undue familiarity.

One must admit that the final step in Matthew's fraternal correction is not realistic in the modern church. The final step (certainly not the very words of Jesus) is to tell the church.

But the institutional church and its officers are the church; to whom is the case to be taken? There have been in recent years several instances that have come to my attention of appeals against bishops to the Holy See. Of all these appeals one knows only that they received Christian burial. The behavior follows quite closely the pattern of the military command when it is charged with faults; it firms up against the outside world. A recent novel, not a big seller, imagined the court-martial of Custer if he had survived the Little Bighorn. In the novel Custer was acquitted. But the outside world here is the church. The problem seems to lie in the false identification of the church with the institutional church—with the hierarchy and, in a lower and outer circle, with the clergy. I wonder why no one, to my knowledge, has not asked whether this organizational state of affairs does not make it somewhat difficult to say, "I believe in *one* holy Catholic and apostolic church."

It is not my intention to lay out a new set of organizational tables, but simply to establish a biblical warrant for fraternal correction of officers of the institutional church. If the institutional church, which pretends to have mastered an extremely complex organizational structure, has been unable to work this clear Gospel mandate into its structure when it has found room for so many things which are clear Gospel mandates, I conclude that it has never wanted to make room for it. It has been careful to preserve its own field of fraternal correction—although one wonders how fraternal the correction of heretics by the rack and the stake was. Perhaps an organization which so long thought of fraternal correction in such terms should have been understandably slow to open itself to the same kind of correction. The failure of the institutional church to institute fraternal correction (can it be instituted?) has meant centuries of guerrilla warfare between the hierarchy and its critics. The warfare has not been Christian, and neither the hierarchy nor its critics can absolve themselves of blame.

The altercation of Peter and Paul in Galatians 2:11-14 is an episode frequently treated because it is unique in the New Testament. The issue was genuinely ecclesial, and it was a question on which honest men had theological differences. It was also an issue which we can be sure aroused much more bitterness in the church than the New Testament has preserved. But that is not why Paul rebuked Peter—and in public; he did not follow the recommendation of Matthew 18:15 (which he never saw) to do it in private. In modern colloquial language, he washed dirty linen in public, he rocked the boat, he made waves, he made a stink. Worst of all, he did not go through proper channels. And why did he do all this? Not because of a theological difference or a dispute over administrative policy, but because Paul thought Peter had failed in candor and honesty; in the words of the New American Bible, he had not been straightforward. And it was not just that; Peter's conduct had offended, indeed deeply wounded, some of his fellow Christians whom he had, to borrow the phrase from Matthew 18, treated like Gentiles or tax collectors (whose low company Jesus was accused of liking). Paul does not set himself up as a model in this episode; he judged that patient acceptance of another's failure to act as a Christian leader would not have been fidelity to his own duty. He did not think Peter was pope or primate (which may create problems for those who think he was), but Paul recognized in him an authority like himself, an apostle; and I have long suspected that most of the authority figures in the primitive church stood with Peter on this issue.

No one need think that Paul's judgment was infallibly right, or that he thought it was. One who thinks he detects a defensive tone in Paul's explanation may wonder whether Paul acted here with the same assurance he shows elsewhere in his writings. If he had maintained a prudent silence, the infant church would have lived down the slur of second-class membership which Peter had cast upon all Gentile converts. It would have taken a few generations, but the welfare of persons is not much considered by those who take the long view of the big picture—that is, the administrative view. The trouble with Peter's blunder, if it was a blunder, was that it made it impossible for anyone to do the right thing. I say if it was a blunder to render the kindness which has always been paid to the man who was first recognized as head of the church— later, if not at the time. But is it a kindness to think that his mistakes arose from a stupid head and a warm heart and not from quite unfeeling calculation? At this distance we have no right to impute either. Peter and the Judaizers have left no written defense of their actions.

How much of the institutional church is due to the even implicit will of Jesus Christ? I suspect that modern critical scholarhsip, following its known consensus on the historical value of the recorded words and acts of Jesus, would say none of it. As practiced by Catholics, critical scholarship has not said that in so many words. In my generation we were taught that it is an article of faith that the Papacy is of divine institution, defined in the First Vatican Council. We were also taught that it is of faith from the perpetual teaching of the church that the monarchical episcopate is of divine institution. To judge from the treatment of these questions in Richard McBrien's recent *Catholicism,* the theses I learned are now in the museum of theological antiquities; how much we age in forty-five years! One wonders whether it is wisdom or cynicism that comes with gray hairs. But if this be the state of affairs which has developed within a single lifetime, it would be extremely rash of me to say anything which sounded at all definite about what Jesus did or did not do to warrant the title of founder of the church. I do not think I can go along with those of my colleagues who say he had no more to do with it than Rabbi Hillel or Pontius Pilate; but if we know nothing of any one thing he said or did, is that not what we are effectively saying?

Based on what shallow thinking I have done, let me venture a few rash observations, and let them stand or fall on their own weight. I have found in the New Testament no trace of any priestly or ministerial class; the books are in a sense anti-clerical. The relations of Jesus with the only religious establishment which he knew are described as mutually hostile; a similar hostility, or at least a lack of sympathy, is described between him and the only thing which passed as a teaching authority. Nothing in his preserved words indicate any suggestion that these authorities should be replaced by others who would do the same thing, only better. He uses them only as examples of how not to deal with religion. To the institutional church all the words attributed to Jesus are religious anarchy.

Yet I believe, and I must believe, that he initiated a movement of human beings toward God. If he did not, we historians have the problem of explaining who did and why they masked themselves behind Jesus of Nazareth, from the point of view of public relations a singularly unattractive figure. That he expressly intended a movement of such growth and duration I cannot say; that he left any directions for such expansion and duration I can safely deny. That the movement he initiated had the potentialities to appeal to every human being of all times and places seems undeniable. If he knew this, he should have known that nothing would inhibit these potentialities more surely than the creation of an institutional structure which would have to reflect the limitations of its time, geography and culture. I will not say that he left to others the task of institutionalizing the movement; this would be a distortion of what we are told about him. I conclude that about any kind of institutional church he said and did nothing. In that sense, and possibly in any sense, Jesus did not found the church, or a church.

The institutional church was created by no one; it grew out of the very human need to preserve the movement which Jesus initiated by the only means which mankind has ever known: organization. Whenever human enterprises are organized, or institutionalized, something is lost of the freedom and spontaneity of the original enterprise. For the institutional church, the problem has always been—and was there when Peter and Paul had their altercation—whether it is preserving what I called the Jesus movement—it might also be called the gospel or the spirit—or whether it is preserving itself. Those who serve the institutional church, and most of its officers serve it well, have never been able to accept the fact that the Gospel and the Spirit will survive even if the institutional church perishes. Jesus does not need the likes of us in order to live; or shall we say that he does need us only as long as we are expendable? God can raise up children of Abraham from these stones.

At least since Constantine, if not longer, the institutional church has been, besides the vehicle of the Gospel, an omnibus carrying many passengers on a first-class ride to power, wealth and worldly security. It will have these riders until the last stop. As long as they are there, other passengers will, like Paul, tell them that they are nuisances to their fellow riders.

Chapter Fourteen

PREJUDICE AND BIGOTRY

IN reflecting upon how to approach this topic, I thought that not everyone who professes Christianity would think at once of the topic as a place where the words of Jesus on love of one's enemies and the forgiveness of injuries are applicable. I thought further that deep personal enmity is not that common in the lives of most people; they rarely, and perhaps never feel consuming personal hatred, the kind of hatred which issues in murder and violence or the infliction of serious personal harm to another in goods or in reputation, the hatred which feels joy when one's enemy is injured or deprived or reduced to ignominy—the kind of hatred which takes its pleasure in inflicting pain or in seeing pain inflicted. I say that it is my impression—and I cannot make more of it than that—that most people rarely experience this feeling, and thus they may think that they do love their enemies, who are that hateful, and that they do forgive injuries, at least most of the time and with some delay. The next thing which occurred to me—and this gives me my essay—is that the New Testament attends to the topic of prejudice and bigotry quite seriously, and that it does treat it as a serious moral problem.

It surprised me when I consulted the *Oxford Dictionary* that neither bigotry nor prejudice is in its definitions directed to persons; they are concerned with beliefs or opinions. Contemporary usage, as far as I am familiar with it, understands the words as concerned with persons at least as directly as with ideas; it is in this sense that I use them in the title of this chapter. I do not attempt to explore the roots of prejudice and bigotry; others, I believe, have done this better than I can. We have learned from such studies that a rational analysis of prejudice and bigotry does little to change these attitudes. Nor do I expect a brief review of what the Bible has to say about these topics to add to the analysis. It will show, I think, that the kind of prejudice and bigotry with which we are concerned is very old, and that its character has not changed much.

We speak of prejudice and bigotry as they are directed to persons for reasons other than personal relationships; the attitude was once well described by a wit whose name I have forgotten as personal dislike of someone whom you do not even know. The Greeks, as usual, had a word for it; they called it xenophobia, which means fear or hatred of foreigners. It is the same root which appears in other words ending in "phobia," and without exception these words all designate an unreasoning response. Perhaps of all of them only xenophobia is given an attempted rational explanation; the attempts fail, because xenophobia is an essentially irrational attitude. All human beings, including ourselves, have unamiable traits; it is not irrational to dislike us for these—although Christian charity tells us to overcome such sentiments with love. But being a "foreigner," that is, a member of some other group than our own, is not an unamiable trait; the psychological need for some rationalization is therefore very great. And the easiest explanation is to attribute to the foreign group as a group, certain unamiable traits, and thus to avoid the necessity of saying that we dislike them because they are different from us. I do not love thee, Dr. Fell; the reason why I cannot tell. But this indeed I know full well; I do not love thee, Dr. Fell.

The ancient world, including the biblical world, knew this human response; it is surely as old as writing (three thousand years B.C.), for we have written evidence for it. It seems neither necessary nor possible to cite particular examples from such an abundance, except for their curiosity. Anti-

Jewish prejudice is often said to rise from Christianity; this can hardly be the reason for its appearance in the world of the Stoic philosopher Posidonius of Apamea (first century B.C.) and the Roman poets Horace (first century B.C.) and Juvenal (second century A.D.). No ethnic gibe ever exceeded in grossness the ancient Israelite description of the Gentiles as uncircumcised. The same Roman Juvenal exhibited an even more virulent prejudice against the Greeks. The poets spoke for the most cultivated levels of Roman society; we may assume that lower levels of education, as they do among us, had their own variety of grossness.

At times the New Testament reflects the peculiar Jewish arrogance toward Gentiles which appears in Jewish writings of the period. It is generally agreed that the words attributed to Jesus do not share the common prejudice; but we cannot dismiss without discussion the story of the Gentile woman and her daughter (Mark 7:24-30; Matthew 15:21-18). The character of the dialogue is, I believe, enough to explain why the Gentile Luke did not include this story. Even her ethnic affiliation is not clear; Mark uses a word found nowhere else in Greek literature (Syro-Phoenician) and Matthew uses an archaic ethnic designation (Canaanite). The response of Jesus to her petition, even after allowances are made for the frankness of popular speech, is harsh and rude; it is certainly out of character with his usual response to petitioners and to those who were social outcasts. What we have is an expression of vulgar anti-Gentile prejudice put in the mouth of Jesus.

To say that we do not have his exact words is a dodge. We never have his exact words, but we discuss the Gospels because they are all we have about what he said. There is, of course, no reason to insist that here, just once, the Gospels remembered and reported his exact words; we have noticed that Luke found them too distasteful to report—or at least that explanation recommends itself. But let us notice that it is not simply a saying of Jesus with no context. The harsh refusal of Jesus becomes the occasion of a duel of wits in which Jesus is worsted. Ancient wisdom was exhibited by the apt quotation of wise sayings, as Jesus here supports his refusal by a proverb. Superior wisdom was shown by capping the proverb, or reversing it, as the woman does. The story makes Jesus himself the butt of the woman's wisdom, and he acknowledges his defeat by granting her petition.

It is all but certain that Jesus never felt the need of explaining why his personal mission did not reach Gentiles. His disciples much later felt the need, and this story explains it— or at least makes an attempt. The point of the story is that any such limitation based on the alleged conduct of Jesus himself is not valid; such a limitation is confuted by what the Gentile woman said to the Lord himself—and he accepted it. If the story is the creation of an expanding Christian community, it comes from the same community which told, or created, the parable of the banquet to which all the neighborhood riff-raff were invited. This story, like other sayings and stories, deals with a Jesus who was known to be as gracious to Gentiles and Samaritans as he was to Jews.

The sacred books of the Jewish community, accepted, as far as we know, by Jesus himself as sacred, do contain perhaps the best founded piece of ethnic bigotry in recorded history. In Matthew's Sermon on the Mount Jesus deals with the Law with what was for a Jew a quite irreverent casualness. One wishes perhaps that he had dealt with this venerable piece of bigotry more explicity, and then one realizes that he and his disciples have been more explicit than Christians have been willing to recognize. I refer, of course, to the stories of the conquest of Canaan in the book of Joshua and the laws of the holy war in the book of Deuteronomy. In the story the Canaanites were totally exterminated by the invading

Israelites and in the laws this extermination is presented as a duty laid upon the Israelites by God.

It is certainly of interest that modern scholarship is convinced that the conquest of Canaan narrated in Joshua is entirely a romantic fiction and that the laws of the holy war are an ideal never reduced to practice. This does not solve the theological problem—although it may raise another —created by a narrative in which a people, represented as God's chosen, are described whether in fact or in fiction as perpetrating the first genocide in recorded history, and as cherishing the belief that this was done under divine inspiration. It does not touch the fact that Christians have often through the centuries appealed to the theology of Deuteronomy and Joshua to carry on wars of extermination. One wonders whether Jesus could have been explicit enough on this topic.

It is abundantly clear that this theme makes it impossible to follow the fundamentalist approach of treating the Bible as a single inspired source of divinely inspired doctrine and divinely revealed rules of conduct. To believe that one should take one and the same approach both to the genocide described in Joshua and Deuteronomy and to the teaching of Jesus is to talk nonsense. One can deal with such problems only by the use of theological criticism. To enter this topic would take us far beyond the topic of this essay, and I have dealt with it elsewhere. Certainly theological criticism runs the risk of misunderstanding. Whatever the risk may be, it is preferable to thinking the slaying of large numbers of people is somehow based upon passages of the Bible. The risk of a critical misunderstanding at least leaves people alive, and escapes the reprimand addressed by Jesus to James and John when they wished, like Elijah, to call down fire from heaven upon some inhospitable Samaritans (Luke 9:54-55). We

Christians believe that Jesus is God's last word. What he is represented as saying makes it totally impossible to incorporate the genocide of the holy war into a Christian life. I observed that Jesus was remarkably casual toward the sacred books of his people. One might say that he was the founder of theological criticism.

Since Jesus was a Palestinian Jew who spent his entire life in Palestine, it is not surprising that his sayings which bear on our topic are directed to the forms of ethnic, national and religious prejudice which were manifested by Jews; I have observed elsewhere that Jesus always spoke to the concrete existing situation, not to abstract generalities. With the exception of the story about the Syro-Phoenician woman, he is uniformly affable and kindly toward "aliens": Gentiles, Samaritans, Roman officers—whom he met in the normal course of his life no more frequently than the average Palestinian villager did; and Palestinian village life did not foster the cosmospolitan worldview. The saying attributed to John the Baptist that God could raise up from these stones children of Abraham could as well be attributed to Jesus himself. It can hardly be derived from the Scribes, although it is dangerous to say that something is not in the Talmud. But such a direct attack on that ferocious ethnic pride which every people exhibits about itself does not sound like the rabbis of the Talmud. It fits the larger pattern which one sees in the sayings of Jesus in which all claims of pride of place and position and even of achievement are denied. If Jesus does not give intelligence or learning or power or wealth due respect, he is not likely to respect anything as trivial as pride of race or nation.

The authors of the book of Acts and the Epistles wrote in and for a Christian community which was becoming a Gentile community; it is safe to say that this process was completed by the end of the first century. The authors of the Gospels, writing in the same community, did preserve the Jewish thrust of the remembered sayings of Jesus, but not without some modifications intended to give the sayings the same immediacy they had in their original form when they were now addressed to a Gentile community. I have mentioned that the story of the Syro-Phoenician woman appears to answer a question which Jesus himself never addressed. But the Epistles were directed to residents of the cosmopolitan cities and towns of the Mediterranean basin, and they speak to our topic as it was encountered in a world quite different from the world of the Palestinian village. The author of the Epistle to Titus (not Paul) quotes a cruel ethnic gibe from a sixth-century Greek poet about the Cretans. It is the type of blanket criticism which we recognize quite well as current among us. But the author of the Epistle quotes it with approval. In an age which we think is more enlightened the appearance of a similar ethnic gibe in a pastoral letter would never be forgiven. As a matter of fact, I have never learned how the modern Cretans feel about Titus 1:12-13. Since we are contemporary with attempted genocide, perhaps we should examine our own delusions about enlightenment. The author of the Epistle, in spite of his ill-mannered line about the Cretans, continues with a program of Christian moral instruction with no hint that he thinks the Cretans are unable or unwilling to accept his instruction.

There are two passages of the Epistles that address ethnic and class differences as obstacles to Christian unity. One passage (Galatians 3:28) is the work of Paul, the other (Colossians 3:11) is regarded by almost all scholars as the work of a member of the "Pauline school." If this is correct, the writer of Colossians seems to have had Galatians as a model; the sentiment is not so frequently expressed that it is a commonplace. Paul in Galatians says that unity in Christ abolishes differences, even the difference between Jew and Greek (Gentile), slave and free, male and female. The author of Colossians asserts the same unity with a longer list of differences: Greek and Jew, circumcised and uncircumcised, foreigner, Scythian (the extreme barbarian), slave and free. It is worth noticing that the line of Galatians echoes one of the "Eighteen Blessings" which the observant Jew recited among his daily prayers; he thanked the Creator that he had not made him a Gentile, a slave or a woman. I do not say that the echo is conscious; I believe that the collection of prayers called the Eighteen Blessings is not attested before the early post-Christian period. The coincidence is striking; the sentiment, if not the prayer, may be much older. No one doubts that the ethnic and social differences mentioned in these two passages were deep. It seems well assured that the earliest Christian churches were assembled just from those social outcasts mentioned so often in the Gospels. It was not just to the outcasts that these words were addressed; they seem directed rather to those who, rightly or wrongly, would never have thought of themselves as outcasts. But the attractiveness of prejudice and bigotry lies in its universal appeal; no matter how low you may be on the social scale, there is always somebody lower whom you can despise. If you cannot accept "Christ as everything in all" (Colossians 3:11), you do not have a Christian community.

I referred above to the existence of prejudice and bigotry in biblical times. But I wonder whether the world of the New Testament, which was the world of the Roman Empire and Hellenistic culture, was not by comparison with our own world a world of broad cosmopolitan tolerance. The Romans had effectively removed political and national differences as a cause of strife. They had also opened opportunities to residents of the Roman Empire without respect to ethnic origin. The number of men from remote provinces and obscure peoples who achieved prominence and success in the great cities of the Empire is remarkably large. When one language (Greek) would carry a man from one end of the Mediterranean to the other, a major cause of division was removed. When a single culture (again, basically Greek) was the arena in which talent contended, the danger was bland uniformity, not ethnic and national rivalry. I simply point out that a number of the things which foster prejudice and bigotry among us seem to have been removed in the Roman peace. This does not speak to the other major social blotches which defaced the fabric of Roman society. It may suggest why the New Testament does not give as much attention to the problem as we think it ought—we of whom some have said that racism is our major social problem. I do not believe that this was ever said of the Roman Empire, under which Galatians and Colossians were written.

I am not sure that racism is our major social problem. In a society as sick as ours has become I do not know what may be our major social problem. In this book we have turned up several which might be adduced as the major social problem, none of which, if solved, would solve all the rest. Nevertheless, if we have social problems which New Testament Christians did not find as acute in their world as we do in ours, it seems that some Christian reflection on these problems is in order—unless we are to say that the Gospel does not speak to them. To this problem the Gospel says that we are all one in Christ Jesus. The question is whether, if we are unwilling to accept this unity, there is any rational or humanitarian basis for that unity of mankind which will annihilate our particular differences. So far no such unity has appeared. We who believe that the salvation of mankind lies in Jesus Christ alone should not think that something else will do the job.

We need to reflect seriously on what bigotry and prejudice have done and are doing to our humanity. About this someone as gifted as Mark Twain should write something like Twain's "War Prayer." Bigotry and prejudice enable us to deal with our fellow human beings as objects, not as persons. When we deal with things it is necessary, in order to control them, to classify them according to types. For practical purposes if you see one Delicious apple you have seen them all— although, when it comes to eating a Delicious apple, it is advisable to look at each individual apple. To think of controlling persons is to deny the dignity and the unique quality of the individual person. When we are classified according to type and so handled—as we are when we are loaded aboard airplanes—we resent it. We complain because we find government agencies and corporations insensitive to our reality as persons, recognizing us only as numbers which identify our type. When we accept bigotry and prejudice, we accept stereotypes for an entire group; and stereotypes mean that we classify them without thought and without experience of the persons whom we stereotype. In fact we reject thought and experience; they might compel us to dislodge comfortable stereotypes long imbedded in our minds which save us the trouble of thought and of dealing with persons as individuals.

Corporations (such as airlines) and government agencies will plead that it is possible to deal with large numbers of people only by depersonalizing them. No doubt this is true; and no doubt this is one of the things which makes civilization a mixed blessing. It seems the price we pay for more things is becoming less as persons. But bigotry and prejudice also serve a useful purpose. They enable us so to arrange our affairs that certain people are treated as means, not as ends. They make it possible to deal with them simply as conveniences—or as inconveniences. They enable us to take self-serving measures which mean for some people sure death, sometimes quick, sometimes slow. They enable us to assure for some people desperate, degrading poverty by depriving them of food, clothing and shelter in order that we might be fed, clothed and housed. It enables us to look with equanimity on children bloated by starvation or wasted by disease or mangled by war and see them as eggs from which the omelet of progress is made. They enable us to be angry at the moral degradation of the victims of the "system," with never a thought that we have excluded them from our "system." We could not do any of these things and retain any claims to human decency if we had to face these people as persons like ourselves, if bigotry and prejudice had not taught us to think of them as things.

Chapter Fifteen

PERSONAL HOLINESS

A correspondent who is also a good friend chided me gently for the apologetic tone which has sometimes appeared in my writing. She did not question my sincerity, but simply observed that one who protested that he did not like to treat certain topics found himself able to overcome his repugnance at length. The point was well taken. And now that I must enter a similar disclaimer about this and the following chapter, I see the same criticism rising again. To say that I feel totally unqualified to write about personal holiness would be meaningless; whom would you expect to introduce a treatment of the subject by a recital of his qualifications? Furthermore, if I find this or some other topics personally so repugnant, why did I not strike them from the list and suggest others? It is probably no secret that the editors let me do almost anything I like. It is true that I have seen over the last—let me see—fifty-four years a number of treatments of this topic which I found revolting. I have no assurance that I am not producing one more revolting item. I have known some people who achieved personal holiness. The trouble is I have a fairly good idea of how they went about it. To point this out seems to grab for the chair of Moses occupied by those who talk but do nothing.

The ideal of personal holiness has been long enshrined in the title of a late medieval classic, *The Imitation of Christ.* In the first two years of my religious training all novices were given a copy of this book with instructions to read it at least for fifteen minutes each day. I am really sorry that the passage of years has eroded the facility I once had of quoting this work for almost any occasion. In recent years the work is

174

less admired for various reasons, not all of them good. It savored rather strongly of that heterodoxy known as Semi-Pelagianism, it expressed a rather self-centered piety, it was obstinately anti-intellectual, and it was more than a bit anti-social; would Jesus ever have said, "As often as I go among men, I become less a man"? More fundamentally, does the New Testament ever recommend in a realistic way that the believer imitate Jesus? Or is the imitation of Jesus a realistic possibility?

Few believers then and even fewer now are Palestinian villagers. To tell people that Jesus is a role model simply bewilders them. Nothing he is known to have said or done recommends him as role model for the father of a family, and still less for a mother; he may indeed have been a model child (except in the anecdote preserved by Luke), but we know nothing about his childhood behavior. There is satisfactory evidence that Jesse James was a model boy. Jesus furnished no role model for one who lives by employment in business or industry, nor for the creative artist, nor for the teacher and scholar. The things which have engaged most of my waking hours during my adult years were things in which Jesus never engaged. Paul wrote to the Corinthians (1 Corinthians 11:1) "Imitate me as I imitate Christ." Certainly the imitation of Christ cannot be achieved by a set of rules. I realize that this may seem to be a rather supercilious dismissal of religious rules, which have a long history as means of reaching personal holiness; and the history is by and large noble. But many founders of religious rules knew that Ignatius Loyola said: if there is no spirit within the organization, rules will not do it. The rule tells the members how to behave as Benedictines or Franciscans or Dominicans or Jesuits, not how to imitate Jesus. Life lived under such a rule will, it is hoped, at least remove some of the grosser obstacles to personal holiness. As we shall point out again below, personal holiness is a personal achievement which cannot be done by someone else on one's behalf.

The teaching of Jesus, as reported in the Gospels, is simple and without subtlety; it is addressed to the mental age of twelve years (as I am told most television programs are addressed). The moral instructions of Jesus, as I have said before, are not hard to understand; they are just hard to do. We have devoted our intellectual subtlety to evading the words of Jesus, or to convincing ourselves that doing something else is just as good and a lot more practical. Matthew's Sermon on the Mount is a collection of sayings of Jesus which deal largely with personal holiness. I am sure that Jesus never delivered this discourse as Matthew wrote it. That all of the sayings were uttered by Jesus himself is in modern scholarship an untenable position. Yet the discourse as a whole is paradoxical enough and exhibits enough of originality, by which I mean independence of rabbinical teaching and tradition, to justify the veneration in which Christians have always held it. Unfortunately the veneration has more often shown itself in admiring exclamations of "Lord, Lord" than in execution (Matthew 7:21). We have created a distinction between the commandments and the counsels (reminding one of a recent witticism about the Ten Suggestions); Jesus, I think, dealt with this distinction (Mark 10:17-30; Matthew 19:16-29; Luke 18:18-30). The man who refuses his "counsel" is said to have excluded himself from the kingdom of God.

A saying of Jesus in this discourse sums up personal holiness by saying that one's righteousness must surpass that of the Scribes (Matthew 5:20); that is, there is no set of commandments of which one can say that their perfect observance guarantees righteousness. In the same discourse Jesus makes not himself but the heavenly Father the model: be perfect as your heavenly Father is perfect (Matthew 5:48). This impossible ideal should be seen in its context. The heavenly Father is the model of perfection in our relations with others. As the Father rains on all people alike with no respect to virtue or kinship or merits or claims, so we should dispense our love to all alike, no matter who they are or what they have done. As I said, it is not hard to understand.

Matthew (11:29) once represents Jesus as presenting himself as a model: "Learn of me, for I am gentle and humble of heart." I believe this is the only Gospel passage in which Jesus proposes himself as a model; but the scope of the model is somewhat restricted. The adjective translated in 11:29 by the *New American Bible* as "gentle" is rendered by the same version in Matthew 5:5 (the third beatitude) as "lowly"— the traditional "Blessed are the meek" of the older English Bibles. I have elsewhere accepted the opinion that the word in both passages represents a social class: the poor, the dispossessed, the powerless, those who are pushed around by the wealthy and the powerful. The word denies self-assertiveness and acquisitiveness, the state and condition summed up by the author of *The Imitation of Christ* as "I am nothing, I have nothing, I can do nothing." May I paraphrase Matthew 11:29 as "Learn of me that I count all your values as nothing"? I said above that I think I have a fair idea of how those whom I have known to have achieved personal holiness managed it. Of all of them I can say that they seem to have completely repressed the instinct to think of themselves. In no situation did this occur to them. They had learned of Jesus that he is, to use the old translation, meek and humble of heart. Ignatius Loyola put it thus in the *Spiritual Exercises* (I am not sure that I quote exactly): Let each one be sure that he will make progress to the degree to which he goes out of his own self-love, self-will and self-interest. May I say once more that it is not hard to understand? It has been grasped, to my knowledge, by some very simple and uneducated people. Jesus is quoted as saying

(Matthew 11:25) that he thanked the Father for revealing to the simple what he had hidden from the learned and clever.

When we turn from the Gospels to the Epistles, we find that personal holiness has a new and somewhat disturbing dimension. This dimension has a somewhat paradoxical quality, and I may confuse my readers more than I enlighten them. Let me state it briefly: the Epistles, especially those of Paul, do not so much call the believers to personal holiness as to become members of a holy community. It is probably unfair to say that much of the existing spiritual literature exhibits a kind of "Me and God" spirituality which does not reflect the New Testament. One of the earliest ways of the pursuit of personal holiness was flight from the world, canonized in the monks of the desert. Earlier I quoted *The Imitation of Christ,* "As often as I go among men, I return less a man." The same author also wrote, "The cell continually inhabited grows sweet." If one wants to match aphorisms, one might say that the farther I flee from men, the farther I get from God. Such an aphorism is at least as well founded in the New Testament as the aphorism of the *Imitation.* Solitude has its dangers too; the greatest is perhaps massive self-interest. Certainly Jesus did not flee the world. He remained in it and overcame it, which is a bit harder to do. In any case few of my readers have the option of fleeing the world; I would say that those who do should not think that flight will solve all their problems of personal holiness.

This does not mean that simply by membership in the church the Christian achieves personal holiness; like guilt, holiness is not contracted by association. It seems to mean that the achievement of holiness for the Christian is never purely personal; holiness is achieved only in company with others with whom the Christian shares both his ambitions and the means by which his ambitions are achieved. The Christian needs the church in order to be holy. He needs it to show him how to be holy. Paradoxically he needs it even if the teaching and the example and the sacraments should fail him. Perhaps one may be pardoned for appealing to the mystical when one deals uncertainly with the area in which human beings come in touch with God. For the church, the community of believers, the community of faith and love, is the present reality of Christ in the world, without whom we have no hope of personal holiness.

For Paul personal holiness—indeed life itself—is identification with Christ, which is not the mere imitation of Jesus or the acceptance of his teachings. Let Paul writing to the Philippians (2:1-11) tell us what this meant to him: you must think like Christ. And how do you do that? Christ, who might justly claim to be equal with God, chose the state of a slave and the humiliation of a death esteemed vile. Jesus spoke of himself as one of the despised and powerless; Paul speaks of him as a slave, and in our western culture we no longer know what the depersonalization of slavery meant—although we make efforts to continue it under other names. As I said, the few genuine Christians I have known seemed to have lost the ability to think of themselves. I will repeat it again until it becomes tedious; it is not subtle. Jesus is quoted as saying that to be his follower one must deny oneself, say that one does not exist (Matthew 16:24). I really do not think I have repeated this as much as Jesus did.

Think like Christ: What will that do to our world of values which we have built up by habit and conviction in our years from childhood, which we have learned from our parents and teachers, from our peers, from our friends and enemies—with whom we share many values—from our reading, from the stage and screen, and now from the omnipresent television? Let us ask ourselves what we think is really important, really worth doing or experiencing, what is to be avoided at all costs? It would shock us, if we went through these things, how many of them have been uncritically accepted, how few are the result of mature thought and conviction. Think like Christ—and how much of what we adore would we have to burn? It is rarely, I believe, that the insight into the gulf which separates us from Christ issues in such a shattering experience of conversion as Paul had. But a movement of conversion, however slow and halting it may be, will sooner or later lead to the awareness that one must deny oneself, say that one is nothing, worth nothing, that to live is Christ and to live any other way is, in the earthy expression of Paul, "rubbish" (Philippians 3:8). When this insight comes, we are as likely as not to go away sad like the rich man in Mark 10:17-27. One needs the support of the church when one realizes that one's life is going nowhere.

One who thinks like Christ enters into the transcendent reality of Christ; he or she becomes a component of the living and active presence of Christ. He or she becomes the full reality of the church. In such Christians others, unbelievers as well as believers, encounter the living Christ. They become channels of grace through whom God acts, and they do this serenely unconscious of what they are doing—because, as I have repeated several times, they never think of themselves. It is not that they have a low opinion of themselves; they have no opinion of themselves. In the modern jargon, they are other-directed. They are so unself-conscious that they do not even carry the normal complement of guilt. If you think of yourself as nothing, you do not think of yourself, nor worry about how you stand in the great ledger up there.

But to return to something I said above: Jesus is not a role model for Christians in the usual sense of the term. I think most of my readers will say with me that Jesus did none of the things on which they and I have spent our adult lives. This has often led to what John Haughey has recently called a "micro-separation" of church and state; since Jesus is not a role model for most of us, we believe that the secular life is its own world with its own models, and that the "religious" or the "spiritual" is another and unrelated world which does not impinge upon the secular—as the southerner thirty years ago said about segregation, religion has nothing to do with it. Therefore have chaplains in colleges, in Congress, in the armed services, but keep religion out of these activities; it has nothing to do with them. One might as well institute a chaplaincy in the Mafia or in a brothel; prayer is one activity, these are other unrelated activities—for which Jesus is not a role model.

One must think like Jesus in order to see how he is to become present in an activity in which he never engaged in a culture in which he never lived. The task may be too much for the individual, and he or she may need the help of the Christian community. But he or she must make the decisions; the community can help, but it cannot manage. An old anecdote is told about a remarkably stupid farm boy whose one skill was finding lost donkeys. When asked how he did this, he answered, "I just figured out where I would go if I was a jackass, and there he was." The simple Christian just figures where Jesus would be, and there he is. This skill would never get him a position in a university department of Christian ethics, but it will solve those of his personal problems which cannot wait for a study in depth by scholars.

Both the Gospels and the Epistles insist that thinking like Jesus is a personal responsibility which each must fulfill for himself or herself. Certainly there are large areas where members of a class will solve similar or identical problems in the same way; there are, for example, medical ethics and legal ethics. Doctors and attorneys both know that in the really tough cases it is not enough to ask what others have done; and I am not referring to what might be called problems of personal holiness, but to problems of professional behavior.

Too often in the modern world we take refuge behind such excuses as "everybody does it." Was it ever different in any society? My friend Gordon Zahn in recent years wrote about a German peasant named Franz Jagerstatter who refused the advice of his bishop, his priest, his neighbors and his family. He stubbornly resisted going along with National Socialism, although "everybody was doing it," and he maintained this position in spite of no more than elementary education and apparently much less native intelligence than many who apparently served National Socialism with a good conscience, or at least a quiet conscience. Of course it cost him his life; he was beheaded. He died having saved something which those who survived had lost; they better than anyone else can tell what that is. I do not know whether Jagerstatter always thought like Christ; he succeeded in doing so at the most critical moment of his life, when millions of others had failed to do so, and his spiritual directors told him he was wrong. I suppose one could say the church failed him; it has been said. But it was the church that empowered him to resist evil; he was not the only Christian who resisted. He is simply an example—and that is why Zahn chose him—of a little lonely man without power and prestige who showed that anyone can think like Christ.

Most of us can thank God that we are not likely to have such a horrendous responsibility of choice imposed upon us. The danger is that, like millions of Germans, we will not recognize the responsibility when it falls upon us. I write as a citizen of a nation which has shown no repentance of the horrors it has done, from the genocide of the American Indians to the nuclear bombing of Hiroshima and Nagasaki and the savaging of Viet Nam. I wrote above of the "micro-separation" of church and state. But at the moment this is not my concern; my concern is with putting on the mind of Christ so that I can make Christian moral decisions in my state of life, my profession, my complex of human relations which is uniquely mine, in which neither Jesus nor any other person is a role model. In my own case, to go no further into particulars, Jesus never lived into old age, and he is not a role model in what are facetiously called the golden years. I mentioned earlier that Jesus was never a seminary or university professor, and he never published a line. As far as our information goes, his relations to the teachers and learned men of his world were generally hostile; they did not like him, and he did not like them. After forty years in this game it is clear to me why he did not like them; I am sure he finds the same things in me. It is also clear why they did not like him; many of my colleagues do not, and for the same reasons—he is a threat to their pride, vanity and self-assurance. I do not want to imply that a teacher and scholar has more of a problem thinking like Christ than anyone else; it is just that I know his problem better. Unless he makes a serious effort to put on the mind of Christ precisely in his teaching and scholarship, he achieves a micro-separation of religion and learning; effectively, he is not a Christian in what he spends most of his time doing. I add, more as a footnote than as a point for discussion, that Jesus was not a priest and certainly furnishes no role model for that aspect of my life. A lot of thought has been given to this, not all of it useful.

Paul invited all of his Christians to reflect on how they might make the mind of Christ a real and effective factor in the management of their lives; otherwise, how could he tell them to do all that they did for the glory of God, even eating and drinking (1 Corinthians 10:32)? How does one make the mind of Christ effective if one is the mother of a family, if one is a physician, an attorney, a banker, a merchant, a salesperson, a mechanic, a factory worker, a soldier, a sailor? Only those who live these lives can tell us. I have enough problems trying to combine the mind of Christ with a life allegedly dedicated to learning to prevent me from telling anyone else how to manage his or her life. All I can tell them is that my sources tell me that it is possible for anyone, that no one is so lacking in talent or education or so underprivileged that the mind of Christ is beyond their grasp.

Are there not ways of life and professions in which it is impossible? It has often been thought so. It is said that the only way one resigns from the Mafia is feet first; I suppose that a life of professional crime should be met the way Jagerstatter met National Socialism. I would hesitate to say that this is the only way of life to be so abandoned. But it is somewhat strange that the New Testament does not often recommend this variety of flight from the world. If the story is true about the composition of "Amazing Grace," I suppose the author felt moved to abandon his career on a slave ship. One can think of many modern ways of making a living which are doubtfully Christian. Further reflection might disclose more, many of which are quite respectable. With the New Testament, I would be slow to make a decision which each person can make only for himself or herself. By his very human existence Jesus put himself in some unsavory positions. Perhaps the mind of Christ is most needed in employments which are not respectable. Unless we are sure we have the mind of Christ in our own way of life, profession or employment, let us be slow to say "A Christian would not do that." Jesus was affable to soldiers, tax collectors and prostitutes. He never told even the Scribes, whom he disliked, that they should give up the profession. That comforts us modern successors to the Scribes.

Chapter Sixteen

PRAYER

LUKE (11:1-4) tells us that Jesus, in answer to a request from the disciples that he would teach them to pray as John had taught his disciples, taught them the Lord's Prayer. Commentators believe that Luke more probably gives the occasion of the prayer, while Matthew more probably gives a more original version of the prayer which is slightly longer and more elaborately structured. The request of the disciples is a bit surprising; they were uneducated men, but they would have heard enough of the Old Testament, which can be called a book of prayer as much as a book of anything else; and the Psalms had by New Testament times become the prayerbook of the Jewish community, from which the Christian community adopted it without change.

The Gospels lead us to believe that Jesus impressed the disciples with what we may call his facility in prayer. This impression should not surprise us; very few people have a facility in prayer. Such a facility was exhibited in the New Testament world by the Pharisees, and Jesus found fault with their exhibition (Matthew 5:5); this suggests that what the disciples saw in Jesus was not the same thing. In Mark 12:40 Jesus speaks sharply of those who say long prayers while they devour the houses of widows (see Luke 20:47). Jesus is quoted (Matthew 6:7) as telling his disciples (somewhat brusquely) to keep their prayers short, remembering that God knows what they need. What Matthew calls "rattling on like the pagans" may seem a bit unfair to the pagans if one remembers from childhood being compelled to kneel for what seemed (and nearly were) interminably long prayers; Jesus gave the Lord's Prayer once, but it took later Christians to think of saying a short prayer fifty times before stopping. We use Matthew's version of the Lord's Prayer rather than Luke's; Matthew's is slightly longer (and therefore better?). The tax-collector is praised for keeping his prayer short, and the Pharisee is not praised for prolonging it (Luke 18:9-14). I cannot forbear pointing out that most traditional Christian devotion has not found much use for one of the sayings of Jesus about prayer quoted several times. If we had been among the disciples who asked Jesus for a lesson in prayer, we would have answered: "Sorry we asked, Lord—we see that we know more about this than you do."

One wonders whether the Book of Psalms known to Jesus contained Psalm 119 with its eight formulae repeated twenty-two times for a total of 176 verses in praise of the Law, which, as we saw in an earlier essay, Jesus praised with great restraint. Of course we know that his Bible did contain that Psalm, and one does not wonder whether he intended to except it from his criticism. One does wonder, but one should not, whether he shared the view of divine inspiration believed by Jews and Christians for so long. As a prayerbook the Book of Psalms has to be accepted with certain reservations; it may be a merely personal quirk, but Psalm 119 says nothing which I wish to say to God on those occasions when I am impelled to speak to him; we shall not discuss how frequently those occasions arise. There are a few other Psalms which I have never been able to use as prayers with any sincerity. Others might say that Psalm 109 sticks in their throat; if you wonder why, I suggest that you read it. The same could be said for Psalm 137. The justly admired Psalm 23 is a rare jewel in a collection which includes more pedestrian verse than do the sonnets of Shakespeare. Psalm 23 follows the directions of Jesus to keep it short. I do not know why it is that when we pray, as when we preach, the less sure that what we are saying is worth hearing, the more certain we are to prolong the effort. It is not only religious speech that is so afflicted with prolixity as a substitute for style and content. I have heard speakers on quite secular occasions who never heard of the old homiletic directive: be brief, be clear and be seated. I have never been sure that Psalm 119—or the Litany of the Saints—does not bore God as dreadfully as it bores me. Neither the householder of Luke 11:5-8 nor the wicked judge of Luke 18:1-5 are the models of God hearing prayer.

There are a few other features of the Psalms, apart from their frequent prolixity, which are less admirable and imitable. It is quite true that the entire position of man at prayer before God is based on an anthropomorphism—more precisely an anthropopathism: the attribution to the deity of human thoughts, sentiments and attitudes. This cannot be accurate; but it is fundamental to biblical religion, and it escapes the more dangerous misconception of thinking that God is impersonal—that is to say, a thing. Prayer presupposes that communication with the deity is possible, that the communication must be interpersonal and that it must be carried on in the only language we know. Biblical religion prefers to run the risk of humanizing God rather than the risk of depersonalizing him. Against this background one may say that the hymns of the Bible, a large number of which are in the Psalms, do sometimes reflect what the critics call the "court style" of ancient monarchies. It takes little theological reflection to see that God does not enjoy compliments, especially if they are fulsome and insincere. The hymn may tell the worshipers something; they should not think that they are telling God something. They need to profess loudly and sincerely, but not extravagantly, that God is good, better than anything else; they should not think that they are adding to his pleasure by their praise. One need not feel doubts about one's religiosity if one finds the language of many hymns saccharine; were it not that I know

God's tolerance is far above mine, I would suspect he finds them such too. An excess of sugar in one's religious language is not the worst thing that can happen in religion. Jesus spoke a good deal about the Father. Either he avoided the language of hymns, or those who heard him missed it altogether.

There is not as much of the element of petition in the Psalms as there is in most popular manifestations of prayer in the Christian community; it is probably fair to say that prayer to most people has meant asking God for something. The Lord's Prayer contains only two such petitions, each as general as possible—a request for the necessary food for the day, and for deliverance from "evil" (or from "the evil one"; the Greek is ambiguous). Jesus himself is quoted as discouraging any specific detailed enumeration of our desires (Matthew 6:8; Luke 11:13). One should not humanize the deity by treating him as uniformed or as uncaring about our needs. One hardly knows how Jesus would respond if asked about prayer for victory in an athletic contest, or for fair weather on a day in the great outdoors. He might suggest that we do not bring God into our self-interest, especially if the concern of our self-interest is essentially trivial. Would he say something similar about prayers for victory in war, found in the Psalms (best commented upon by Mark Twain in "The War Prayer"), or for success in financial deals? He might warn against making God a partner in our evildoing. As I remarked above about the prayer of adoration and praise, no Christian can seriously believe that God needs to be informed about our needs, or cajoled into granting our requests, like a weary and impatient parent. In petition too we are telling ourselves something: that we depend absolutely upon God for everything we are and hope for.

If we humanize God by thinking of him as a tired and impatient father, it must be admitted that in prayers of petition we often appear to be spoiled whining children, who have learned no word except "Gimme." The book of Psalms, which is a handbook of liturgical hymns and prayers, was never meant to be read all at once; but even in small doses it often comes through with a complaining tone, to which one might readily apply Isaiah 7:13 (not written to this situation). Self-pity is not a pleasing note in prayer; it is often present, and the Psalms have plenty of it. It is found in the words of Jesus about prayer. Paul tells us that when he permitted an expression of self-pity to escape him in prayer, he received a short and unsympathetic answer from the Lord (2 Corinthians 12:7-9). An old and once popular hymn has become a target of that, as it deserves: "Nobody knows the troubles I've seen, nobody knows but Jesus."

One may also notice in the Psalms a note of self-righteousness which occurs too frequently. If we think that Jesus knew the Psalms reasonably well, he can hardly have been unaware that the parable of the Pharisee and the tax-collector (Luke 18:9-14) could easily be taken as directed at such prayers as Psalm 26; 44:18-27; 101; 119 (previously mentioned); and 139:19-24. Up to a few years ago, when those who were obliged to recite the Roman Breviary were obliged to recite Psalm 119 several times a week, more than any other Psalm, I thought that even in Latin it did something to the soul. One can explain the religious-cultural background of such liturgical professions of innocence in ancient Israel and in early Judaism, but one does not so explain their survival, nor anything like them, in a liturgy which professes to derive ultimately from the teaching of Jesus. The prayer of the tax-collector was not repeated 176 times running.

In the remarks attributed to Jesus which I have more or less summarized here, there are no sayings which concern community or liturgical or public prayer. We know that this played a large part in Jewish piety—in fact, one might say that it was Jewish piety. Jesus seems to have accepted that the disciples would be normally "pious" in the sense that they would take a normal part in cultic prayer. He warns them only against ostentatious and insincere piety. From occasional words and phrases we conclude that when the Palestinian Jew addressed God privately, he took a posture which left observers in no doubt what he was doing. Jesus warns against this (Matthew 6:5-6). Probably even private prayer was always vocal and audible; in this sense all prayer was public, addressed to God and to anyone else within hearing. The Epistles show that the early Christian communities adopted forms of common and public and liturgical prayer similar to the forms found in Jewish and Hellenistic-Roman religion. Many written formulae of these religions have survived; they indicate not only that the language of prayer is nearly universal, but also that the economy recommended by Jesus is a radical departure from conventional language in any religious society.

Prayer, like other activities of the Christian life, is an activity to be carried on by the members of the church within a Christian community. I have mentioned earlier that the individual moral responsibility of the Christian person cannot and should not be met apart from the Christian community. Christian prayer is uttered "in Christ," which means in the body of Christ which is the church. The security of the Christian when he approaches God is not the security of the writer of Psalm 26 nor of the Pharisee of the parable of Luke 18:9-14, but the security which rests upon his identification with Christ and with the Christian community. Not every expression of liturgical piety is to everyone's taste, nor has it ever been; but the Christian who thinks he or she does not need the concrete existing church in order to pray, or that he or she does it better alone, has some things to learn about who Jesus Christ is, what the church is, and who he or she is. We have to bear one another and forgive one another even when we pray together. I cannot imagine Jesus saying that the noise of others praying bothered him at prayer. Common prayer is one of the ways in which we Christians discover each other, even if we are not always sure about finding God. Any believer knows that the petty grudges, angers, envies and hatreds which he habitually cherishes stop his mouth if he attempts to open it in prayer; if he really prays, he must purge himself of what he knows displeases the God whom he approaches as a suppliant. Christians know what Jesus meant when he said that if you cherish a grudge, do not even attempt to pray until it is settled (Matthew 5:23-24). Prayer, even the basic community liturgical prayer, reconciles us to each other.

I do not find much in the New Testament about that kind of prayer which is called contemplation; perhaps I did not look thoroughly enough, but the topic is certainly not as easy to find as the love of one's neighbor or the renunciation of wealth or the refusal of violence. I have said that the context of the Lord's Prayer in Luke is a request that Jesus would teach the disciples how to pray. He did not accede to this request in this context or in any other by instructing them in the practice of contemplative prayer. Perhaps they were not up to it; but Teresa of Avila, who probably knew as much about the topic as anyone, seemed to think that everyone is equally up to it—or equally not up to it. Jesus is said once to have spent the night in prayer (Luke 6:12; the *New American Bible* glosses this somewhat as "communion with God"). Neither this passage nor any other suggests that he did this every night. The millions who have fallen asleep at meditation should be comforted to read that, at a time when almost everyone would be awakened by terror, if not moved urgently to prayer, Jesus fell asleep—in a storm-tossed open boat (Mark 4:38; Matthew 8:35). Sometimes Jesus prayed, and sometimes he fell asleep.

Someone has written—I cannot place the source—that no prayer of Jesus is more precious for us than his prayer in Gethsemani (Mark 14:32-42; Matthew 26:36-46; Luke 22:42-46). Apart from Luke's comforting angel, the Gospels agree that the three witnesses thought they saw him overcoming a tense inner conflict (an "agony") caused by the prospect of some great pain which he would have preferred to avoid. One has to ask some questions. How much did the disciples witness, when they confess that they were so drowsy that they could not stay awake? What might have been the object of the inner conflict? Jesus did not tell them. Such inner conflicts are often the occasion of deeply sincere prayer, but not always; sometimes they drive people up the psychological wall. In any case, regular prayer which arose from such an inner conflict would attest a rather disturbed mind. Furthermore, whatever be one's Christology, at the minimum one believes that the personal relation between Jesus and his Father is not shared by others. The episode of Gethsemani is indeed precious, for it shows that even Jesus knew the very human agony of uncertainty, all the more agonizing when it cannot be shared. I am not sure, however, that it makes Jesus a role model on how to cope under such circumstances. I am even less sure that his behavior in what, if it happened to us, we would call a spiritual crisis, is a model for regular prayer.

It is now almost twenty years since I included in a book a chapter in which I made some remarks about contemplative prayer and the contemplative life. Limiting myself to observations based on biblical books, I thought my observations were careful and modest; I learned from some readers that they were not careful or modest enough. I remarked above that Teresa of Avila seemed to think that contemplative prayer was within the reach of anyone who wanted it seriously enough; I may add that what she meant by a serious desire is enough to put it out of reach for most Christians. She did observe—and I do not quote exactly—that contemplative prayer is not a reward for virtue achieved but a means for growth in holiness. She also warns against the dangers of self-deception and insists on the need of direction and counsel, passing the often quoted remark that if she had to choose between a holy ignorant man and a less holy learned man, she would go with the learned man. The remark is often quoted as if she implied that learning and holiness cannot be found in a single person, which she never meant. We may grant that the combination is rare. In any case I recommend that any who are seriously interested in pursuing the topic of contemplative prayer should read such classics as Teresa of Avila, John of the Cross, Francis de Sales and our recently deceased Thomas Merton. They may find these works heavy going; I said above that what Teresa of Avila thought was a serious desire is too much for most people. On this topic I make no pretense to speak with expertise; I speak about it only because silence about the topic might be misconstrued to signify that it has no importance.

I will risk saying that there is more contemplative prayer in the church than most people know, but that it is rarely recognized as such, and that it is no more than fleeting glimpses of the reality of God. That I find is the best description of what is called contemplation. If Paul experienced contemplative prayer—that is what 2 Corinthians 12:1-4 seems to imply—he says that what he experienced cannot be put in speech. Teresa and John of the Cross say the same thing, but they make the effort anyway; and they fail. One is suspicious when one hears the revelation of God described in too much detail; personally, I do not believe it. Jesus himself suggests that the only real test of Christian contemplation is Christian performance; I may so paraphrase Matthew 7:16-20. Yet Paul says that even if one surrenders one's body to be burnt, and has not love, it is nothing (1 Corinthians 13:3). Christian performance, I have often said, is simple, but it is deceptively simple.

Prayer, especially contemplative prayer, has long been defined as familiar conversation with God. But how does one know that one is talking to God and not to oneself? How does one know that there is two-way communication? The history of Christianity is loaded with people who were sure that God spoke to them. From a position of second-guessing, however, we know that whoever spoke to them was not God. St. Ignatius Loyola, writing from a year of experience of the solitary life of contemplation, wrote some rules for what he called the discernment of spirits, no doubt recording some of his own history of false starts and bad leads. He never recommended to his followers that they should repeat his experience for themselves. Yet he insisted that they should experience a remote imitation of the experience, under direction (which he had lacked), and make a prolonged serious effort (lasting a month) to clear their minds of anything which might be worldly interest or self-interest. The theory was that a mind clear of other things would be open for God.

Leaving the theoretical question open, it is clear that such a program of mental and spiritual housecleaning is not within the reach of most Christians, and Ignatius Loyola never thought it was. Nor did he think it was universally necessary for Christians who wished to be Christians. He thought that those who experienced such a program undertook a responsibility to the church and to their fellow Christians to do things which those who had not had such an experience could not do. There is some elitism here, but I think it is tolerable: from those who have more, more is demanded. Ignatius never thought that this kind of *noblesse oblige* lay only upon himself and his company.

I have degressed somewhat on Ignatius Loyola and the *Spiritual Exercises* because of his attempt to organize Matthew 7:16:20. No one denies that principle, and no one thinks that only Ignatius Loyola fulfilled it. Apart from revelations, many of which are as phony as a three-dollar bill, prayer is supposed to bring one into closer union with God. This is true even of community petitions and community hymns, which may become routine. It is even more meaningful when prayer issues in a greater awareness of the reality of God, under whatever aspect that reality is perceived either anew or for the first time. It may come either from prolonged reflection or what seems to be sudden insight. I mentioned that such knowledgeable people as Teresa of Avila and Ignatius Loyola were convinced that it could be produced by submission to a regular and rather rigorous discipline. But even they would admit that ultimately there is no book for it. I think it was Teresa of Avila who said that few even among contemplative religious reach contemplative prayer because they are afraid of it. Do we not all fear knowing God better than we do? A glimpse of the reality of God is a glimpse into the nothingness of self. Better not look.

Chapter Seventeen

THE ROLE OF WOMEN
IN THE CHURCH

TO one of my age it seems that the position of women in the Catholic Church has suddenly become a topic of heated controversy. It takes little reflection to see that the controversy is heated largely because it is long overdue, but not solely for that reason. It is heated also, and perhaps equally as much, by willful blindness to reality and the insensitive refusal to deal with women as persons manifested by many members of the hierarchy and by my fellow priests, including the Supreme Pastor of the faithful. I suppose some will think that a decent respect for the supreme authority should impose silence on me when the supreme authority talks like a fool; to paraphrase a figure from American public life recently deceased, he is the only pope we have. That is the reason why cruel folly in the Supreme Pastor is intolerable; silence is certainly cowardly, and may be sinful. This does mean that one must accept with the same silence the boorishness of Mary Daly; women like Anne Carr and Mary Jo Weaver, to take only two examples because they are personally known to me, make their point with much more cleverness and depth and without the bad manners. One may say that John Paul II and Mary Daly deserve each other.

I have learned from experience that to speak on this controversial topic at all is certainly to say something that will offend someone. In my first paragraph I have already gotten a few of the targets of offense out of the way. Of all the topics in this book, this one furnishes a better excuse for retaining a prudent (or cowardly) silence. Yet I choose to deal with it because I believe that no Catholic can refuse to reach a personal

196

decision on the question. I have made my decision, and I am sure enough that it is right to present it here, although I know that it is not above criticism; most of the criticisms I have heard. What I intend to do here is to set forth some—and only some—of the biblical reasons for the decision I have reached. The position I have adopted is not rigid; it can be modified by further reading and discussion. But there is no chance that I will withdraw from the position that the Catholic church has not attained the fullness of its reality as Catholic and as church until it reaches the condition described by Paul in Galatians 3:28: there does not exist among you male or female; you are all one in Christ Jesus.

One may adduce evidence from the text of Paul's letters to show that not even Paul himself always wrote and acted according to this ideal; this is a fact which we must face. But I wish people (like an indignant lady who recently wrote to the *National Catholic Reporter*) would not charge Paul with things he never wrote, like Ephesians and the First Epistle to Timothy. The science of biblical criticism, chancy in spots, is at least as well-established as the philosophy of equal rights for women. One must accept that the same Paul who wrote Galatians 3:28 also wrote First Corinthians 14:33-36. There are explanations, but to indignant women they will sound contrived; so for the moment let us say that Paul had trouble achieving consistency in thinking about women and dealing with them, as all men do. Women are not inclined to forgive this, possibly because of the innumerable proverbs (all masculine) in several languages in the spirit of *La Donn'e mobile*. When Paul wrote the lines from First Corinthians, he echoed his Jewish-Hellenistic culture. When he wrote the lines from Galatians, he struck an entirely new Christian note, not previously heard in any culture—and surviving unheard in Christian culture.

There are no reported words of Jesus which touch the

question directly. Jesus has also been faulted for his failure to speak directly to slavery. I have adverted in earlier essays to the fact that Christians have succeeded in ignoring many of the problems to which Jesus did speak directly. But I believe even the more radical members of the women's movement do not find fault with what is reported about the dealings of Jesus with women. He may be the only historic figure whose preserved words do not echo the simple and unspoiled assumption of male superiority. As I have remarked, Paul echoes it (although he rose occasionally above it), and the other biblical books of Old and New Testament echo it. Male superiority dominated human culture from the dawn of recorded history in Egypt and Mesopotamia, through the empires of the ancient Near East, through Greece and Rome, through the development of western Christendom and Moslem civilization. One talks about it as one talks about the weather. It is all the more remarkable that the unskilled writers to whom we owe all the remembered words of Jesus presented him as dealing with all human persons simply as human persons—a presentation which they were incapable of inventing, as most readers of the Gospels have been incapable of believing it.

If Jesus did not address this question directly, some of his quoted remarks are revolutionary if applied to the position of women in society. They have not been applied because they have always been read against the background of male superiority. I was sharply reminded of this after a recent homily in which I spoke of the dispute of the disciples about who among them was most important (Mark 9:33-37). A disturbed parishioner told me that his wife had understood my remarks about self-assertion as directed to women, who, she thought, need and have long needed to assert themselves. I had not thought of this application. Now that I am reminded, I could have specified that the words of Jesus make no distinction of sex, and that self-assertion in my limited observation is a masculine rather than a feminine vice. It causes discord whether it is found in men or in women. Jesus is not on the side of the masculine assertion of superior importance.

This observation puts me in a position not friendly to the statement issued by the Holy See under the late Paul VI on the ordination of women. Like many, I found this statement unfortunate. It is simply impossible to cite the New Testament as a document supportive of male authority. I say this in spite of the few statements made by some New Testament writers, which any woman theologian can cite at the drop of a biretta. Interpretation is rarely a simple matter. But it can be said without doubt that the New Testament, and still less Jesus himself, never proposes men as the only fit subjects of holy orders, and women as unfit subjects. In the New Testament holy orders are conferred upon no one, male or female. The apostolic church was a church of the laity. Since ordination is clearly an ecclesiastical institution, no doubt ecclesiastical authorities are empowered to determine upon whom it should be conferred. I feel no obligation to justify and defend their policy of selection, especially when it seems to reflect a pre-Christian sexism rather than Christian unity.

What was the role of women in the apostolic church? It does not seem that either Galatians 3:28 or 1 Corinthians 14:33-36 describes it; it was not the Jewish community, in which only males were Jews, nor was it the eschatological church in which people neither marry or are given in marriage (Luke 20:34-35). Even Paul would have had trouble explaining the submissive silence imposed upon women in 1 Corinthians 14:33-36 to women he knew like Priscilla (or Prisca) and Phoebe. Priscilla is mentioned in Acts 18:1-3, 26; Romans 16:3; 1 Corinthians 16:19. She is never mentioned apart from her husband Aquila, nor is Aquila ever mentioned apart from her. Paul calls them his helpers without distinguishing between the two, and gives both of them unusually high praise. They are his fellow workers in the service of Christ Jesus. Phoebe is recommended to the recipients of Romans 16 (who may not have been the Romans). She is called a deacon of the church (or minister), the same term which Paul applies to himself and others. The "deaconess" of English versions is a gratuitous bit of sexism. One concludes from the rather full mention of Phoebe that Paul thought her worthy of respect and wished others to share the sentiment. It seems to be entirely unjustified to suppose that the "help" she gave to many, including Paul, was limited to what we think are the traditional "feminine" offices of serving males. If you read the Bible as sharing your prejudices, you can find them.

Romans 16 contains a list of 25 names in addition to Phoebe to whom Paul sends greetings. Since it seems unlikely that Paul knew so many people personally in a city which he had never visited, many scholars have suspected, for this and other reasons, that the last chapter of Romans was added to the copy of the letter sent to another church, probably to Ephesus. Of the 25 names six are clearly feminine, not counting Junias and Olympas; the ending "-as", which has misled some, is not feminine, and Junias is joined with the masculine article and adjectives. Of the six Prisca (Priscilla) is called a fellow worker. Mary, Tryphena, Tryphosa and Persis are said to have worked hard for the Lord or for you. Again, there is no reason in the text or the context to infer that these services, singled out for commendation, must be the kind of services which we in our masculine wisdom have defined as feminine. In fact Aquila and Priscilla appear to have formed an early evangelical team, to use a modern expression.

But let us make the extreme supposition, that the seven women whom Paul mentions shared in every feature of the apostolic ministry, but that the universal custom of the apostolic church, attested by Paul, forbade them to speak in the assembly. In this hypothesis several points must be noticed. In the first place, I do not think that Paul meant or implied that the spirit comes only to men; he may have, and several of my contemporary fellow clergy believe it, but it seems out of character with Paul. If the spirit did speak to a woman, Paul would have to say that she should give the communication to her husband and let him pass it on to the assembly. This rather obvious absurdity must have struck Paul, and it must have struck the Corinthians as well. Paul's treatment suggests that what he calls a universal practice (was it?) was more often breached than honored. It must be noticed that Paul does not appeal to any word of the Lord in support of the custom of the churches, as he does elsewhere; he appeals to "the Law," from which he says at length elsewhere that Christ has liberated us from its yoke. He might have done well to follow his own principle here; scholars have been unable to find any text in the Law which Paul could have had in mind. For a rabbi this is sloppy homework. In not appealing to Jesus, Paul shows a better understanding of Jesus than the Holy See under Paul VI, which did make such an appeal. I said or implied that any man who ventures to speak about this topic runs the risk of making an ass of himself, one reason why I would just as well let it lie. I believe that I can say that Paul in this passage speaks as a Jewish rabbi, as he does in many other passages, and that he himself furnishes the material from which we can correct him here.

It is often and carelessly said that Galilean women accompanied Jesus and "ministered" to him. It is rather strange that the one episode in which Martha invited Jesus to a dinner which she had prepared for him has been built into a career of "ministering" to Jesus, and women have for centuries been praised in the church for accepting the "role" or the "lot" of Martha. In fact Jesus does not praise the "lot" of Martha. In a saying which is doubtfully original her concern with his personal service is rather put down. Perhaps those who have so long praised the "lot" of Martha were quite aware of the putdown. Such brutal frankness, if it represents a genuine memory of the words of Jesus, can be understood only in the context of unusually close and familiar relations between Jesus and Martha—which the traditonal "role" of Martha implicity denies. Several women friends have assured me that a male guest who spoke of their hospitality in these terms would not be invited to share it again. They may understand Jesus better than Luke did. The story of the "lot" of Martha can be transmitted only in a culture which assumes without discussion that the supreme fulfillment of women is to render services to men. One need not know the Gospels very well to know that Jesus asked for personal services from no one, and said that his destiny was not to receive such personal services but to render them. If this saying were taken seriously, it would play hell with male superiority.

Let us, then, leave the non-existent ministering women and the non-existent role of Martha out of the discussion. The story of Martha and Mary does show that the words of Jesus are addressed to women as well as to men. Many of my fellow churchmen have long implied that many of his words are not addressed to women. If the Congregation of the Faith wishes to issue another doctrinal statement, let it enumerate those maxims of conduct and those forms of Christian service or "ministry" from which in the Gospels women are explicitly or by definition excluded. Tell us what Jesus told us to do that can only be done by men, and tell us just where he said it. Let it be made clear beyond doubt that the Congregation is not interested in preserving a cultural structure of male domination—Machismo, I believe this position is vulgarly called. Let us examine that structure and see whether it is defensible in Christian terms at all by those who profess allegiance to one who rejected domination of anyone by anyone. I am tempted to make some rash offers for every text clearly defining male roles as dominant and female roles as subordinate and so understood by the majority of biblical scholars; but I am serious, and such an offer, I fear, would not be taken seriously. But if anyone wishes to enter into correspondence on the question, he will find me willing to put my money where my mouth is, as long as he will do the same thing.

It seems incomprehensible that the Catholic Church, not always submissive to Jesus' teaching on the search for and the use of power, the pursuit of wealth and the radical denial of self-aggrandizement, has almost completely failed to apply these principles to the relations of men and women. One may view the ministry of Jesus, to be carried on by the church, as a ministry of reconciliation; this phrase would not be the worst one-word summary of the mission. That the mission of reconciliation is imperfectly achieved and that there is still much to do need not be shown. Possibly one of the reasons for the failure of the church to be the agent of reconciliation between God and man and between man and each other has been its stubborn refusal to accept the mission of reconciliation between men and women. Because it has been an agent of strife and contention in this basic field of human relations, its voice for peace in other areas has been hollow and thin. At the heart of its institutional structure it has defended a power center which is oppressive and divisive. Its sincerity as a peacemaker is questionable. It has refused to treat half its members as full human beings and as members of the body of Christ in whom the Spirit dwells. It has perverted the ecclesial structure to support a power clique. Only recently did I abandon phrases like "for us men and for our salvation" and "this blood shall be shed for you and for all men." The Latin from which these phrases are translated does not distinguish gender here. But the mistranslation expressed the underlying belief that if men are saved, everybody is saved. Male superiority denies full humanity to women, just as slavery was made possible only by denying full humanity to the slave.

And now let us return—for the last time—to Paul's attestation of the tradition of the apostolic churches that women should not speak in the assembly, and his somewhat gratuitous addition that they should learn from their husbands—or from their fathers; even at Corinth there were unmarried women in the congregation. Paul's meaning is quite clear, although I have expressed my doubts that this saying represents his consistent practice; but I cannot prove anything. My question is whether this common practice of the apostolic church is to be imposed upon the church for all generations to come. God knows that we have departed far enough from the practices of the apostolic churches in so many respects that one must admire our stubborn adherence to them here—where, as I pointed out, Paul adduces no word of the Lord to justify the practice. The apostolic churches had no pope, no cardinals, no archbishops, no cathedrals, no canon law, and no "apostolic bank," to pick a few examples out of a hat; it did not even have priests. Where the church has wished, it has treated apostolic traditions with great freedom. Is it respect for apostolic tradition or respect for male supremacy that appears here?

In a church fundamentally Jewish in origin and in a world culture where the role of women in government, business and the arts was—shall we say—uncertain, it is not hard to understand why the primitive church had some trouble finding a role for women. I have suggested, following many of my colleagues, that it found a much fuller role for them than the later church has recognized. It should be plain that the limited role of women was determined not by the natural law —whatever that is—or by the words of Jesus, but by the culture in which the church was immersed: what the Gospel of John calls "the world." In this, as in other respects, the church struggled long and persistently to change the culture, with more success in some areas than in others. Even in the area of male-female relations it slowly produced some changes. Is it not time that the social and biological theories of male domination should be given the same Christian burial given (not without struggles) to the primitive natural sciences which were implicit in the thinking of every New Testament writer? But the Holy See has made it clear that without further pressure it will continue to consider the role of women as determined by a cultural framework long dead.

I am not suggesting that the position of women in the church should be determined by the cultural patterns of the twentieth century anymore than I am suggesting that it should be determined by the patterns of the first century. Faddism is no more attractive than archaism. I am observing that the church should follow the Gospel—the whole Gospel —in determining the position of all its members. Cultural patterns and moral patterns are hopelessly interwoven, and it takes some discernment to distinguish them. I know that Jesus in his treatment of people refused to be trammeled by the cultural patterns of the Hellenistic-Roman world or the religious patterns of Palestinian Judiasm. The church has shown far less freedom in dealing with the contemporary culture. With reference to the position of women in the church, it has simply not developed an authentic Christian position; it has reflected the ways of the world.

Those who suggested this topic meant, I think, that I should address myself to the role of women, not in the church, but in the modern world. It does not pain me to confess that I am not equal to the task. Perhaps the church is not equal to it either. But the church can clean its own house. It can show the world a church community in which women are fully human and wholly free. It is sad that the same Holy See which has spoken so eloquently and, many think, so wisely, on behalf of the poor and oppressed, and in addition has spoken in behalf of peace, has added its voice to those who speak and act for the oppression of women. I have suggested that this may be the reason why the church has not been an effective agent of reconciliation. I have confidence that the Spirit will move it. Could the church but bring itself to recognize that its mission, like the mission of Jesus, is to human persons without regard to sex—I may add race or previous condition of servitude—and grant to all its members a fully responsible part in its ministry without any distinctions based on purely worldly and human considerations, it would have freed itself of the last vestiges of an antiquated pre-Christian social structure. It would do something which perhaps more than anything else could free it from the world of sin to be what it has never been, fully the church. I remember a saying of the Cambridge classicist, F. M. Cornford: the only reason for doing the right thing is that it is the right thing to do; all other reasons are reasons for doing something else.

Chapter Eighteen

PRIESTHOOD AND VARIETIES OF MINISTRIES

EDWARD Schillebeeckx, the author of two massive volumes on Christology, has more recently presented a slender volume entitled *Ministry: Leadership in the Community of Jesus Christ.* I can make no better recommendation to anyone who is seriously interested in the topic of this chapter than to read this book. Those who might have been frightened by the weight and the depth of *Jesus* and *Christ* should not be discouraged; this is a book of only 165 pages, of which 142 are text. Many readers can easily omit the pages of notes. It is true that Schillebeeckx, unlike me and some others, is incapable of shallow theological writing. But while the book is dense, it is always clear; for those who are willing to make the plunge, it affords them a view of a first-class mind equipped with more than the necessary learning engaged with the real problems of life in the modern Catholic church, with concern and total candor. I recommend no books, including the Bible, without reservations; if Schillebeeckx were to read this book, he would have noticed a few points of divergence. His books will enrich the minds of others, as they enriched mine. It is only fair to say that this brief chapter has been affected by Schillebeeckx more than by any other modern writer; but I do not wish to blame him for the ideas I set forth. For them I take full responsibility.

It is no secret that the Catholic priesthood is in deep trouble; and since the church depends on its priests for so much of its ministry, the church is also in deep trouble. The depth of the trouble may be seen in the reluctance of the institutional church to recognize the problem. When some of us priests gather, it is a commonplace to observe that we are survivors of a dying breed. This is not true, at least not yet, in countries which only a few years ago were mission territories supplied with priests from Europe and North America. They are not ready to return the favor, and I am not sure that most of the parts of North American which I know are ready to receive it; but they had very well better get used to the idea. Cities which I knew well thirty years ago now have one priest or none in parishes which used to have four or five. If I were bishop in such a diocese, I would feel like the captain of the *Titanic.* Yet no alarm is manifested. The institutional church seems to regard this as a temporary passing phenomenon, like a business depression. This may be a pose. But the passing phenomenon will last long enough to relieve me of worry over whether I shall have to eat my words.

The simple fact is that we of the vanishing generation are not furnishing examples—role models in the contemporary jargon—which young men wish to follow. If I could tell why, I would write a book. If it takes the time and talent of a great many good men to write the book, it should be written, and with more honesty than one is accustomed to see in church-sponsored studies. I must add that if it were written honestly, experience justifies the fear that it would be suppressed; and that in itself may show some of the reasons why we are not attractive role models. To how many people in the modern world is the priest the image of a kept man? I am sure —and I should know—that this is a false image. I know also that many men in all walks of life are willing to be kept men. If the take is good enough, it is surprising—or perhaps not surprising—how many men can be bought. The priesthood has had its share of such. But I have known enough priests to know that whatever brought them to the priesthood and kept them there, it was not the take.

I must note—because Schillebeeckx does not—that in my

generation and earlier the decision to become a priest was in many cases—I hesitate to say most—a childhood decision which was carried unchanged into adult life. By accident I happened to make an adult decision the year I was ordained. To be fair, the opportunity was always there; to be fair also, the alternative was always presented as a character failure. I think these childhood decisions were rather ruthlessly exploited, but I could be wrong. I wanted to be a locomotive engineer long before I thought of being a priest. In a town where the railroads at that time employed 4,000 men, becoming an engineer was more realistic than becoming a priest. Had I followed my earlier childhood dream, I would now be a retired member of another dying breed. One of the more hopeful signs of the future is that the seminaries and the novitiates are no longer admitting boys. One thinks of Plato, who believed that in an ideal system of education no one would be admitted to higher education before the age of thirty-five. Like many things Plato said, it deserves thought.

Schillebeeckx and others assign as a reason for our failure to furnish role models the fact that our role is archaic. I do not know that Schillebeeckx put it so baldly, and I certainly ought to be more guarded in language; but he leaves no doubt that the role of the priest in the modern church is as antiquated as the soutane over knee breeches, black stockings and buckled shoes which only a few yers ago were the only accepted clerical garb in most European countries. I cannot in this brief effort go into this vital question at length, and it is unnecessary since so many others have done it so well. But I can suggest that those who are serious about the problem should inform themselves to the limit of their ability on what has been said and that they reflect seriously on what it means to them and what it may demand. How serious should we be? To return to my illustration given above, the Catholic Church may be the Conrail of the ecclesiastical world. We are concerned with the question of staying in business.

I can summarize much of what Schillebeeckx and others have said by saying that the priestly mission in the modern world suffers from being clericalized. I believe a friend said years ago that there is nothing more pathetic than a priest who has become an anti-clerical. Pathetic or not, I am compelled to ask myself whether the status symbol which I have enjoyed for forty-three years corresponds to anything which we can find in the words of Jesus Christ, whether authentic or attributed to him by the evangelists. I am aware that that status symbol at some times and in some places was a certain sentence of imprisonment, exile or death. These times, let us face it, have been rare. In most of my life where I have lived it has often meant "We have a place for you, Father" or "We have a special price for you, Father." Knowledge of how this privileged position often struck others at times made one wish that consideration could be less effusive. I was warned once that I should not mention my status to an automobile dealer; he had a special price for doctors and priests, a little higher than he charged anyone else. Good for him, I thought then and still think. I realize that the professional religious person seems necessary for the business of the church in modern times. Jesus and his disciples make no appearance as professional religious persons. Paul seems to have approached the professional religious person, although he was professionally a tentmaker and a volunteer religious worker. If the modern professional religious person had or claimed no more status than Paul seems to have had, I think we would be spared much of our trouble.

The clericalization of the ministry has meant that anything which is deemed proper church ministry is limited to a small group of male celibates who form possibly the world's largest club—in which, let the laity clearly know, not all the members are of equal standing. The club treats non-members, women by definition and married men, as fringe members or hangers-on. Some years ago I wrote a few words which some others have liked on the freemasonry of the Catholic priesthood. I have enjoyed it, and I am sure it is a major sustenance in what can be a very dull and discouraging life. The freemasonry is international and intercultural. Since it is woven of shared experiences which cannot be duplicated outside the group, no one has ever felt the need for expanding the structure so that married men and women could share this fellowship. It is not strictly a religious fellowship, but it is not secular either. And much as I have enjoyed it, I fear that I now see it as a pleasing and perhaps necessary byproduct of an unwholesome social structure, not entirely unlike the *morale* of a gang. I said then that a priest leaves the freemasonry by becoming a bishop. Only one reader objected, a friend then recently become an auxiliary bishop and since become head of a large archdiocese and sure to be created a cardinal. For his sake I regret that I said it, although I still believe it, and I would be glad if he were to prove me a liar. I said this because I thought that priests are not sure that their loyalties are the same as those of bishops. If this is true, it deserves reflection. I would hate to see the freemasonry of the priesthood perish, because I believe that, with all its faults, it represents an excellent example of Christian fellowship. There seems to be no way of saving it except to enlarge its membership beyond the male celibate club—in fact, to make the whole church like the fellowship of the priesthood. In the church we are not together, and the archaic clerical state may be a major factor of division. It is worse than archaic.

We must also consider that by definition the priest is a cultic officer. This has long caused difficulties. For most of my forty-three years I have been a hyphenated priest, a priest-teacher or a priest-writer or a priest-scholar (at least in effort). There are many other things which can be hyphenated with priest. All of them are full-time professions or occupations which need no justification to be done, and if done properly, they seem to leave the hyphenated one no time to be a priest. But if no time is required to be a priest, what does a priest do? The hyphen is offensive to both sides of the pair; we do not speak of a husband-teacher or a husband-writer or a husband-scholar. Men used to speak occasionally of a woman writer or a woman scholar (no hyphen) as though it were remarkable that one person could manage to be both (with ever so slight a hint that if she was a woman, she could not be much of a scholar, or vice versa). I have long suspected that the same ever so slight hint was present in such designations as priest-scholar, meaning that if he is a priest, he cannot be much of a scholar. It may also mean that he is not much of a priest; I have spent too much of my life hiding behind Thomas Aquinas, and I am now old enough to wonder why anyone ever tried to combine two totally demanding vocations which cannot but interfere with each other. I suspect Thomas Aquinas did not manage the combination very well either, considering the writing he had done before he was fifty.

Yet the New Testament church knows no cultic officers, nor would anyone deduce from its structure that the cultic officer would become the controlling officer in the church. In several passages the New Testament enumerates several "offices" or "ministries," and the cultic officer is not among them. These different offices may and probably did intersect at times in single individuals; that does not seem to be important. Nor do the authors of the Epistles attempt to rank them —an example which contemporary church officers would do well to follow. Paul says that they are nothing without the "gift" or the "office" or the "ministry" of love. I am reminded of a bishop who read something I wrote and, I was told by a correspondent, asked whether I thought he had to love everyone in his diocese. He is dead now, and it is too late to tell him Yes, that is just what I meant. It goes in my office or ministry too.

Yet the modern priesthood is very inadequately described as a cultic office. In fact so much is laid upon the modern priest that he often despairs at the simple magnitude of the demands, for most of which he has no preparation and for which there can be no preparation. We were all trained in the seminary to preach and to sing high Masses; the training was an assurance that when necessary both would be done, but it was no assurance that either would be done well. The priestly ministry can be conducted only by a ministerial team, ideally trained in special skills. For some of these skills experience supplies; schools, after all, are the only places where beginning teachers can acquire experience. Such teams are not likely to be found where the cultic officer treats religious educators as cheap unskilled labor and not as sharers in the ministry. This is not a matter of titles or salary or recognition of roles, but of that gift without which Paul says all other gifts are empty. I do not know how many priests enter church ministry for gain; and since they seem to be smart, I do not see how there can be any. I do know that this entitles no one to exploit them as if they were an old coal mine.

It should be clear from what I have said so far that I have learned to respect my fellow priests who are priest-priests (if we must use the hyphen) profoundly. If they do even half the work they are supposed to do, they are meeting demands which I never had to meet. One who knows both sides of the hyphen always respects the other side. There is no "ministry," there are "ministries"—different gifts but the same Spirit, an early Christian said. In the modern church there seems to be a need and place for teachers, scholars and writers. For these offices there seems to be no need for ordination to a cultic ministry. If the ordination is present, it may impede the work of the teacher, scholar and writer. The impediment comes because some other ministers do not respect the ministries of teaching and writing, not from the very nature of these ministries. The same can be said of other ministries, but it is better said by those who are engaged in these ministries. I wonder if contempt can be shown more deeply and sincerely than by treating another as irresponsible and incapable of any decisions more weighty than the decision to button one's clothes and to blow one's nose.

I have said that the apostolic church was a church of the laity—or, if one prefers, a church of the clergy. Paul states as clearly as could be stated that the church has no distinctions of rank or status (1 Corinthians 12:27-31, for example; other passages could be cited). Paul had never heard of a community which was all chiefs and no braves, but he seems to address one. Every member has a ministry, and that ministry should be respected and cherished. Whether it is set off by ordination or some other rite seems unimportant to Paul. But when one compares, even in the new ritual, the pomp and solemnity of episcopal consecration or priestly ordination with the simplicity of baptism and confirmation, there is no doubt that the ritual is saying something. I am not sure that Paul would want that said, even by ritual.

I have long thought that the New Testament and the New Testament church eliminated the sacred, in the ancient and still usual sense of the term, from religion. I realize that if what I say about priesthood and the ministry depends upon my ability to establish this thesis, I will raise more objectors than I can handle. But the New Testament knows no sacred places, sacred objects, sacred rites—or sacred personnel. Paul tells the faithful that their bodies are the temples of the Holy Spirit (1 Corinthians 6:19). I do not wish to trivialize the Eucharistic ministry, but the New Testament nowhere tells us who presided at the Eucharist; it seems clear that the person was not designated by cultic ordination. The New Testament church was a storefront church; no doubt it could not afford to be anything else, but was it improved when it was enriched? I can therefore state my personal conviction, which I am sure is not shared by all students of the New Testament, that whatever was esteemed sacred was a quality with which all the members were endowed. There were no sanctuary railings in the apostolic church.

Hence I am not sure that the modern question of what is or is not suitable priestly conduct is relevant to the ministry. If it is based upon an archaic distinction, it is not. The question is whether conduct or dress or manner of life is fitting for a Christian, not for a priest. In our dispensation marriage is unfitting conduct for a priest. I do not wish to be carried from my point by this controversial question; but I see where I would have to go. In most European countries it has long been the rule that priests are suspended (forbidden to exercise their priestly powers) for attending the theater or the races. This penalty was traditionally and quite legally avoided by leaving one's diocese to attend the theater or go to the races. In the early church the prohibition of attending the theater and the races (and in earlier times the gladiatorial games) was imposed upon all Christians. It was retained for the clergy when the faithful were released, no doubt on the grounds that the clergy ought to be or at least appear to be a little better than the rest of the faithful. This is where I wonder if we have not somehow lost touch with the New Testament. I think, for what my opinion is worth, that there are some forms of spectacle or entertainment which are unfitting for a Christian, clerical or lay. I suppose only a few would find fault with the prohibition of the gladiatorial games. Only students of the ancient world know how raunchy the Roman theater had become in the Empire.

The Second Vatican Council (and I do not have the exact

reference at hand) recommended that the "secular" should be the area where the laity should be the responsible Christians in action. I wonder whether this does not need further study. Father Robert Drinan was more or less pontifically ordered to resign from the United States Congress. A few years ago another Jesuit (whose name escapes me) was not ordered to resign from the staff of President Nixon's speech writers. I do not know that either was engaged in any activity unfitting to the clerical state. Being a member of the House of Representatives or of the President's team of speech writers is no more unbecoming to the priestly state than anthropological or linguistic scholarship (and less likely to get you in trouble than theological scholarship) or managing the diocesan or monastic finances. I am concerned that the Holy See wishes Drinan, because of his priesthood, not to exercise a right accorded him by the constitution of the republic of which he is a citizen. It is simply a question of power, as it often is and should not be. If the Holy See can instruct the clergy not to hold public office, what keeps it from telling them how to vote or not to vote? Nothing, as far as I can see, except the absence of a will to that effect. And my readers should know, if they do not, that I have a blind spot for politics, which I regard as the world's second oldest profession. The fact that I have experienced no worthy practice of politics in my life in the civil society, in the church, or in private organizations does not prove that there can be no worthy or decent politics. It does not encourage me to hope that anything can be accomplished for the mission of the church by politics. The risk of great loss, attested by experience, I find is far greater than any tenuous good which might be expected. The use of politics is exactly on the same moral level as the use of war on behalf of the mission of the church. I do not expect everyone to believe this, and those, whether lay or clergy, who think differently will use politics for church purposes. I am sorry, but I must remain detached from their activities.

Nothing of what has been said is to be construed as meaning that there is no place in the church for professional religious workers; these appear in the apostolic church, and they were paid. The New Testament does not support the formation of a caste of professional workers, who think that the church belongs to them or that they are the church. The rise of a clerical caste has deprived the church of the diversity of gifts which Paul said that the Spirit promises (Romans 12:6-8; 1 Corinthians 12:28). The ministry suffers because a narrow base of selection deprives it of openness to the needs and the possibilities of performing the ministry in other than the safe established ways. All founders of religious communities had to struggle with the inertia of the safe and approved way. We have enough experience to see that the limitation of the professional personnel of the church to male celibates does not give it enough persons for its needs. My experience has been that being adult, male and celibate qualifies one for nothing.

Chapter Nineteen

SIN

THE late President Calvin Coolidge was celebrated for his taciturnity, a trait which his successors might well have studied more closely. An anecdote told that when he was asked what the preacher had spoken about at the Sunday service, he answered, "Sin." When further asked what the preacher had said about it, Cal said, "He was agin' it." As I sit down to attack this topic, I am worried that Cal may have said all that can be said and all that has ever been said about sin. I do not know that anyone has ever come out flatly and unambiguously in favor of sin, except perhaps Macbeth, but he is a fictitious character. The genius of Shakespeare makes this fictitious character say explicitly and without weasel words just what he is after. But Macbeth's candor comes as the climax of a dramatic development which portrays a moral breakdown. As theater Macbeth goes; as a portrayal of how a wicked man acknowledges his wickedness, it does not go. My problem, which permits me to take the topic further than Calvin Coolidge did, is whether the contemporary world can accept Macbeth as good authentic theater. And why? Because I am not sure that many of my contemporaries admit that human wickedness exists.

Perhaps this is too unsympathetic a summary of most modern thought as it is expressed in literature and what passes for the arts; and I shall do well to set forth the impressions from which this summary has been, without plan, assembled. Let me be brief on various forms of determinism which appear in modern discourse; most of it is not systematic, and I am not sure how many people are affected by it. But there are many of the learned fraternity (and their views filter down into popular belief) who seem to think that the power of free choice is a delusion. In one way or another some inner compulsion drives us to what is now called antisocial (not sinful) conduct. If this is the proper understanding of human behavior, then of course sin is an archaic concept, a superstition, just as virtue is. Just as sin should not be punished, but treated, so virtue should not be rewarded— but what? Those whose compulsions drive them to socially acceptable conduct are also compelled to treat or to incarcerate the antisocial. I appeal to an agnostic for his famous observation: William James wrote that anyone who has resisted temptation knows that he possesses free will. I will draw no conclusions about the experience of determinists with temptation. If anyone really believes that moral good or moral evil is entirely beyond his or her reach, I suppose I have nothing to say to them. I would not want them as teachers of my children, if I had children. Nor would I want them as attorneys or judges. If I were charged with a crime, I should want them on my jury.

Those scholars who believe that determinism is an established principle, should this fall under their eyes, may feel that I have unfairly dismissed it. I do not believe in it, and I know I shall not be forgiven for taking it as seriously as they take the ideas of sin, guilt and responsibility. Jesus Christ, and a large number of wise men before him and since him, have accepted the reality of sin. If there is no sin, Jesus obviously accomplished nothing and left no savings of any value. If there is no evil except the evils of poverty and disease, about which Jesus effectively did nothing, then it is a dangerous and damaging waste of time to talk about him; and those who think that he and those who call themselves Christians are tilting at windmills can be understood if they echo the words of Voltaire: *Ecrasez l'infame*. Much good could be done with the resources which Christianity has devoted to the pursuit of wind.

It should be obvious that I cannot share this view; and over the years of my life I have gradually become convinced that sin is not only a real and genuine evil, but that it is the only evil (apologies to the late Mr. Lombardi). At the risk of sounding snide, I will say that those who think that something other than sin, meaning human malice, is wrong with the human condition have lived lives so sheltered and protected that they have simply never encountered evil and looked it in the eye. Since very few can be so sheltered and protected from human experience, I am forced to conclude that they have refused to recognize the unpleasant reality; they have met Dr. Jekyll and refused to see that he is Mr. Hyde.

The first thing we have to admit is that wickedness more often than not brings us much that is profitable and agreeable. Let us be extremely cautious and slow to say that what is profitable and agreeable is also wicked. The good life which is presented to us as a political, social and economic ideal is impossible without wickedness. To borrow a phrase, you cannot make an omelet without breaking eggs. So many of us have really never encountered evil because we were protected from discovering that it was evil. This has been going on a long time; Isaiah (8th century B.C.) announced woe to those who call evil good, and good evil (5:20). Look at the omelet, not at the eggshells. Look at the prosperous and peaceful communities of the middle and western United States, and not at the unmarked graves of Pottawatomi, Seminoles, Cherokees and Sioux.

This can go on quite a long time, and the recital is as wearisome to the reciter as it is to the reader. I said in an earlier essay that we in modern times can hardly move about without bumping into something which has been made available to us by the death, impoverishment or physical and moral destruction of the innocent and the helpless. We know this; but we attribute it, I said, to that impersonal mythological reality we call the System, which replaces God in the minds of most citizens of the modern world, even in the minds those who think they believe in God. They do not; they believe in Mammon. Some years ago I wrote of this topic and I called it radical evil. I encounter this when I hear good men and women explain pathetically that the United States had to drop the atom bomb on Hiroshima and Nagasaki, and should drop it again if it has to. If he were available, I am sure that Hitler would be explaining that he only did what he had to do, as Churchill would be saying the same thing about Dresden.

And this is about as close as I can come to the favorite contemporary cop-out for sin: It is not we, individual men and women, who commit sin; society is the sinner. This is much like what is called in literary criticism the pathetic fallacy, the attribution of human thoughts and sentiments to non-human subjects, such as the raging sea. The attribution of sin to society is not quite the pathetic fallacy, because society is human. Nor is it another fallacy, the attribution of concrete real existence to an abstraction—such as "War is cruel." What society lacks is identity; you cannot find an agent for what is done by society, and I do not mean a responsible agent. No one can be charged with guilt or blame for what is done by society, except society; and this is to say that what is done by society is not done by anybody, and the inaction of society is nobody's failure. According to the adage, everybody's business is nobody's business.

The abstraction which is society is formed from concrete reality; if it were not, it would be what is called in logic a figment of the mind, an imaginary invention like the griffin and the unicorn. I doubt that many contemporary thinkers would accept my statement that to blame society for what is wrong with the human condition is just as valid as blaming it on the devil. The abstraction which we call society is not like the abstraction which we call nature; the personification of nature is a mythological way of speaking which one would think beneath scientific language. The personification of nature is formed from the perception of a reality which is beyond our control, at least at this stage of evolution. Should we evolve far enough, we will no longer have to say, "It's not funny to try to fool Mother Nature." But society is not a force like Nature (Mother or something else); society is the reality of the people who compose that society, or it is nothing. I should add that it includes all those who have composed the society; for the society is largely determined to be what it is by what it has been. It cannot escape its collective memory (another pathetic fallacy) as found in its history, its achievements, its failures, its traditions, its mores and folkways. The society wears its past like a medal and carries it like Marley's money-box, it is both its beauty and a loathsome disease. It presents us with our opportunities and our capacities as well as our limitations, our ideals as well as our weakness. It is the past which makes us speak of society as if it were a force of nature beyond our control. Is it also true that society determines our present and our future?

If it does, let us drop the Gospel and proceed immediately to the reformation of society, for there is no other hope for the human condition. The Gospel does not move toward the reformation of society; it addresses the individual person. In modern times it has been criticized for an excessively individualistic morality and a failure to perceive or to recommend action about evils which dwarf the individual and can be properly seen only on a social scale. If one attends to the actual proclamation of the Gospel as it has been done, there is some validity to this criticism. But I have yet to hear of a genuine social evil, by which I mean a condition which appears to be completely beyond the reach of the individual person, to which the Gospel does not speak. If my mail should now point out some obvious things I have missed, I will be glad to incorporate them in a later effort. But I do not quarrel with the view that society is the largest obstacle to the exercise of free human choice of the good, that society is the greatest tempter, to use an old-fashioned word, in our experience. The Gospel reminds us that we are society, and that when we shall have reformed the political structure and the economic system, we shall still leave society unreformed. We may not say to the mythological being called society, "You have made us wicked; now make us good." This kind of remark we might expect from the Moral Majority. My observation has been that most social reforms and planners do not differ from the Moral Majority in philosophy, strategy or tactics; they differ only in the moral precepts they wish to impose.' Right wing or left wing, they are all compulsive, and they make me sick.

The Gospel recognizes that society has no reality beyond the reality of the human beings who compose it, and who ultimately give it what character and what direction it may be thought to have. This is not to deny that human beings in the mass do display a force which differs so much from the force of each individual member that it may be said that the total is more than the sum of its parts; sociology is not physics or mathematics. But the social force is not a force of "nature," nor is it superhuman; the ancients often deified social forces as they deified natural forces. The theist thinks they seriously misunderstood both nature and society as well as the deity in such mythologizing. The fallacy, as I have said, lies in the implicit assertion that the individual person is powerless against social evil. The gospel proclaims that the individual person can overcome sin and death by his or her personal union with Jesus Christ. How this is realized in particular instances could be the theme of a discourse much longer than this. I referred in a previous essay to Franz Jagerstatter's refusal to submit to the certainly massive social evil of National Socialism. I do not think that anyone would care to say that those who saved their lives by yielding reached a higher human fulfillment than he did, or that he could not have used the words of Charles Dickens' hero: It is a far, far better thing that I do than I have ever done. I do not know whether the modern ideal of fulfillment as self-satisfaction can accept martyrdom, not only as fulfillment, but as possibly the only way to retain some elementary human decency. I fear the modern idea of fulfillment is to avoid discomfort at any cost, even the cost of elementary human decency. And thus the Gospel ideal of resisting evil even to the point of pain has become irrelevant. Change society, but not the standard of living. Perhaps one cannot be changed without changing the other.

The deceptive prospect of achieving good by changing the society instead of changing individual persons is deceptive on two counts: It demands less from the individual person, and it promises a quicker return for the trouble taken. The speed with which social evils have been eliminated in modern societies suggests that the promise of quick change is false; I can say no more, lest some disputant throw at me G. K. Chesterton's celebrated remark about Christianity: It has not failed, it just has not been tried. This is true of Christianity, which did not so much overcome Roman civilization as reach a compromise with it. The bastard issue of that compromise was Christendom. But one may always suggest some new social nostrum for the ills of society, until one reaches the last and most desperate remedy, the surrender of personal freedom to do evil or good. A planned society is still a human phenomenon; its only peculiar trait may be that it shows the humanity of the planners rather than that of the planned. May not the planned society be the contemporary version of the forbidden fruit of which it was said, You will be like gods, knowing (that is, controlling) good and evil? The result of eating the forbidden fruit was the discovery that the eaters were naked.

We may therefore look again at the biblical mythology of sin. Paul in Romans (chapter 5) made the myth of Paradise the controlling myth in the traditional theology of sin. Because no one outside of the fundamentalist Bible belt now believes that Adam and Eve were real persons like David and Bathsheba or that the events related about the forbidden fruit and the serpent have any more historical value than the story of Snow White and the Seven Dwarfs, we easily treat the myth of Paradise with the same seriousness with which we treat biblical astronomy, geography, physics and medicine. I have said elsewhere that myth deserves to be taken seriously as an attempt to make it possible for human beings to live with reality without going up the wall. The myth of Oedipus as handled by Sophocles or the myth of the family of Atreus as handled by Aeschylus or the myth of Medea as handled by Euripides are universally agreed to express genuine insights into the human condition, even though they are historically as valuable as the story of Snow White. I quoted above an insight into the reality of life found in the words of a fictional character, Sydney Carton. The Bible has long been thought to contain many such insights into the reality of life, perhaps as many as *The Origin of Species* or *Capital* or *The Wealth of Nations,* none of which are strong on astronomy or physics or medicine.

I said that Paul made the myth of Paradise the controlling biblical myth of sin. The book of Genesis contains several myths of the origin of sin in chapters 4-11, not to mention other books. All of them express, but not with equal subtlety, the beliefs expressed in the myth of Paradise. These may be thus summed up: Sin is universal in humanity, from its origin; it affects the innocent as well as the guilty; it is entirely the fault of man, not to be attributed to factors beyond human control. It is not at all clear that these myths or their use by Paul express the belief that sin is hereditary. These beliefs do not depend upon the historical character of the story in which they are told, just as Sydney Carton's assertion that it is a far better thing he does than he has ever done can be rationally discussed without any reference to the historical or fictional character of the narrative.

When Paul uses the myth, he adds to it the belief that sin is not only universal but inevitable and invincible, that it is beyond the power of human beings collectively (in society) or individually to overcome. As universal and inevitable threats to human welfare he places sin and death on the same level. He believes, and this is the central truth in his proclamation of the Gospel, that only Jesus Christ has delivered man from these twin perils, and that human beings can choose the freedom and deliverance which Jesus offers them rather than the bondage to sin which they have chosen. It is clear that I read Paul in modern times as presenting freedom and deliverance from the bondage of society; perhaps my colleagues in biblical studies will say I should have left out that precision. I am not sure that we understand, when we deal with Paul and the Gospels, what unworldly means. Like society, the world is an abstraction; but from what reality is it formed?

But we may leave that question hanging in the air. When Paul speaks of sin as universal and inevitable, he speaks of the internal pressure which in theology is called concupiscence; and he comes close to calling this a determinant, so close that many of his readers have so understood him. But he affirms the possibility of deliverance from "this body of death" (Romans 7:24) through Jesus Christ our Lord. A force from which one may choose to be delivered is not a determinant. Luther and Calvin, in Roman Catholic views, exaggerated the power of sin over the individual person—or rather, they underestimated the saving power of God in Jesus Christ. But neither they nor other Reformers ever thought of saving their contemporaries from sin by denying the existence of sin. I said above that if sin is not the basic evil of the human condition, then Jesus Christ lived and died for nothing, and he left no teaching of any value on the realities of life and death, of which in this hypothesis he was totally imperceptive. This imperceptive rabbi was quoted as saying that all the evil that men do comes from the heart, which he spoke of in the usual biblical sense as the seat of thought and emotion. He showed no awareness of the possibility that there might be nothing wrong except a deprived background or a glandular condition. As Paul does, Jesus attributes the element of compulsion, which almost always appears in evil-doing, to the person's thoughts and desires. In a strange way, Jesus and Paul might have accepted the grain of truth in a rather silly popular song in which the singer boasted that he had done it "my way." So did Adolf Hitler and Charles Manson. But to say that it makes a difference what you do, whether you do it your own way or some other's way, is to fog up the question with moral considerations.

Too much concentration upon the reality of sin may not be as bad as ignoring it or denying it, but it is depressing and discouraging. Paul's pairing of the inevitable and invincible twins, Sin and Death, tends to make one mythologize them into superhuman and supernatural forces, an anti-God which even God cannot subdue. Yet this is just what Jesus tells us not to believe. If one believes in the reality of God under any aspect at all, one believes that God is more powerful than evil; in the biblical faith sin is a human work. If one believes that the existence of God is meaningful to us at all, one believes that God communicates this power to us. If one believes that Jesus has more meaning and value than Mickey

Mouse, one believes that Jesus has revealed the reality of God and the meaning of human existence. This is what Christians have always believed, however they may have misconstrued their belief. I suggested above that Christendom was an illegitimate offspring of Christianity; but it preserved a distorted belief that Jesus Christ is the most important factor in human existence. Because of that belief, even Christendom could exhibit examples of human victory over sin. These men and women showed the possibility of refusal to be trophies of the world in its war against God.

The number of men and women who have succeeded in living truly beautiful lives has never been great, but it is a larger number than we realize. When one encounters them, even secular humanists will not dispute that their lives are beautiful, that they have shown the meaning and the value of human existence and the possibility of human fulfillment. We all admit that their lives are beautiful; but we would rather lead lives not quite so beautiful, but of what we think is more assured comfort. In such of our fellow men and women the Gospel has borne fruit a hundredfold. Society, no matter how well planned it is, can offer no one, not even its most gifted and endowed members, more than what the Gospel offers all, even the most underprivileged: Go and do likewise.